2009-2011

Elementary School
Test Materials

ISBN-978-1-105-03933-1

2009-2011 Elementary School Test Materials

Table of Contents

Thank you for purchasing the 2009-2011 mathleague.org test series. Good luck to you and your students as you prepare for this year's math contests! Upcoming tournament information and the latest mathleague.org policies and information can be found at our website, http://mathleague.org, and you can reach us at mathleague@mathleague.org or 1-866-387-6284.

mathleague.org is eager to help bring local math contests and championship meets to areas where such opportunities do not currently exist. Feel free to contact us if you would like more information on hosting a local contest or setting up a mathleague.org championship in your state or province.

This page intentionally left blank.
[sic]

Elementary School Sprint Test 11021

Problems 1-30

Name: _____

School: _____

Grade: _____

Correct: _____

Incorrect: _____

SCORE (5 x Correct - 1 x Incorrect) = _____

Scorer's Initials: _____   Scorer's Initials: _____

DO NOT BEGIN UNTIL YOU ARE INSTRUCTED TO DO SO

This round of the competition consists of 30 problems. You will have 40 minutes to complete the problems. You are <u>NOT</u> allowed to use calculators, slide rules, books, or any other aids during this round. If you are wearing a calculator wrist watch, please put it on the end of the table now. Calculations may be done on scratch paper. Record only the letter of the answer in the blanks in the right-hand column of the competition booklet. If you complete the problems before time is called, use the remaining time to check your answers.

<u>Scoring</u>: Five points will be awarded for each correct answer. One point will be deducted for each incorrect answer. No deduction is taken for skipped problems.

1. Ava's 10th birthday is this year (2009). What year will be her 16th birthday?
   A) 2014   B) 2015   C) 2016   D) 2025

2. Today is Saturday. What day will it be 165 days from now?
   A) Sunday   B) Monday   C) Tuesday   D) Wednesday

3. Rolf's pet kangaroo eats 2 bags of kangaroo food per day. One bag of kangaroo food costs 45 cents. How much does one week of kangaroo food cost Rolf?
   A) $0.90   B) $3.15   C) $6.30   D) $9.00

4. 9 tens plus 3 hundreds plus 4 ones equals
   A) 934   B) 394   C) 349   D) 493

5. Which is the following is evenly divisible by 9?
   A) 1233   B) 1234   C) 1236   D) 1239

6. Two prime numbers are added to each other. The result can **NOT** be:
   A) 14   B) 13   C) 7   D) 3

7. Pei-Chan had 1 quarter, 2 dimes, 3 nickels, and 4 pennies. His mother gave him three dimes, one penny, and two nickels. How much money does Pei-Chan have now?
   A) $1.05   B) $1.01   C) $0.87   D) $0.79

8. One-third of $(3 + 6 + 9 + 12 + 15 + 18 + 21 + 24 + 27 + 30)$ = ?
   A) 165   B) 110   C) 55   D) 330

9. In the land of Ah-oooga, 2 Oogies is worth 3 Boogies, and 5 Boogies is worth 7 Noogies. How many Oogies are worth 21 Noogies?
   A) 6   B) 7   C) 9   D) 10

10. What is the value of $(12 \times 12 \times 12) \div (4 \times 4 \times 4)$?
    A) 27   B) 12   C) 9   D) 3

11. Which of the following polygons has the most sides?
    A) hexagon   B) octagon   C) pentagon   D) rectangle

12. One week, three days and five hours is how many hours?
    A) 101   B) 135   C) 216   D) 245

1. _____

2. _____

3. _____

4. _____

5. _____

6. _____

7. _____

8. _____

9. _____

10. _____

11. _____

12. _____

Elementary School Sprint Test – 11021 © 2009 mathleague.org

13. What is the sum of the remainders of (9876 ÷ 5) and (1234 ÷ 10)?
    A) 0　　　　B) 1　　　　C) 5　　　　D) 10

    13. _____

14. (The sum of all the digits of 2009) x (The sum of all the digits of 2010) =
    A) 33　　　B) 0　　　C) 22　　　D) 36

    14. _____

15. Eleanor makes a big brownie in a rectangular pan with length 10 inches and width 14 inches. She then cuts the big brownie into little square brownies with area 4 square inches. How many little brownies does she get?
    A) 6　　　　B) 25　　　C) 35　　　D) 70

    15. _____

16. This year, Teresa is 10 years older than Evelyn was 2 years ago. Evelyn is 6 this year. How hold will Teresa be in 3 years?
    A) 21　　　B) 17　　　C) 15　　　D) 13

    16. _____

17. Which of the following is the largest?
    A) 3/8　　　B) 4/10　　　C) 5/12　　　D) 6/14

    17. _____

18. How many days are there in the months of July, January, November, and June, combined?
    A) 121　　　B) 122　　　C) 123　　　D) 124

    18. _____

19. What is the value of (5 + 6 + 7 + 8 + 9 + 10 + 11 + 12 + 13 + 14 + 15 + 16 + 17 + 18 + 19 + 20)?
    A) 200　　　B) 210　　　C) 220　　　D) 250

    19. _____

20. 3 squares with perimeter 8 centimeters are joined, without overlap, to form a rectangle with length 6 centimeters. What is the area of the rectangle?
    A) 4 sq cm　　B) 8 sq cm　　C) 12 sq cm　　D) 24 sq cm

    20. _____

21. At the math contest snack bar, one cookie costs $0.49, one lemonade costs $0.99, and one sandwich costs $1.99. Together, Jorge and Mateo buy 2 sandwiches, 4 cookies, and 2 lemonades. They split the cost of the food equally. How much money does each of them pay?
    A) $4.00　　　B) $3.99　　　C) $3.98　　　D) $3.96

    21. _____

22. What is the value of (9753 x 8427)?
    A) 82188531　B) 82188551　C) 82188571　D) 82188591

    22. _____

23. A 3-digit palindrome number is a number which is the same whether read front to back or back to front. For example, 636 is a 3-digit palindrome number. How many 3-digit palindrome numbers are there that are less than 300?
A) 9   B) 15   C) 18   D) 20

23. _____

24. Jasmine has 7 coins, which are pennies, quarters, nickels or dimes. She has at least one of each coin. What is the difference between the smallest amount of money Jasmine could have and the largest amount of money Jasmine could have?
A) $0.27   B) $0.44   C) $0.72   D) $1.26

24. _____

25. $2009 + 2008 - 2007 + 2006 - 2005 + ... + 4 - 3 + 2 - 1 = ?$
A) 2009   B) 3013   C) 4009   D) 4013

25. _____

26. Don had a whole number of marbles. He gave one-half of his marbles to Betty, then gave one-half of the marbles he had left to Joan, then gave one-half of the marbles he had left to Peggy. At the end, Don had 4 marbles left. How many marbles did Don start with?
A) 8   B) 16   C) 32   D) 64

26. _____

27. What is the hundreds' digit of the product (999,999,999 x 777,777,777)?
A) 7   B) 6   C) 3   D) 2

27. _____

28. Vanessa is thinking of 3 different whole numbers, each less than 50. She adds them together. What is the largest possible value of the sum Vanessa gets?
A) 144   B) 147   C) 148   D) 150

28. _____

29. For every 10 cookies Joon buys, the cookie shop takes $2.00 off the total cost. Each cookie costs $1.75. How much money does Joon spend when he buys 25 cookies for his class?
A) $46.50   B) $43.75   C) $39.75   D) $35.00

29. _____

30. How many two digit numbers have a ones' digit that is larger than the tens' digit?
A) 27   B) 36   C) 45   D) 54

30. _____

Name: _____

Grade: _____

School: _____

SCORE: # 1 _____

SCORE: # 2 _____

Scorer's initials _____   Scorer's initials _____

DO NOT BEGIN UNTIL YOU ARE INSTRUCTED TO DO SO

This round of the competition consists of eight problems. They will be presented to you in pairs. Work on one pair of the problems will be completed and answers will be collected before the next pair will be distributed. The time limit for each set of the two problems is six minutes. The first pair of problems is on the other side of this sheet. When instructed to begin, pick up your pencil and begin working. Record your final answer in the designated space on the problem sheet. All answers must be complete, legible, and simplified to lowest terms. This round allows the use of calculators, and calculations may also be done on scratch paper, but no other aids are allowed. If you complete the problems before time is called, use the time remaining to check your answers.

Scoring: Ten points will be awarded for each correct answer. No deduction is taken for incorrect answers or skipped problems.

1. Abigail has a clock that is too fast, and a clock that is too slow. The fast clock gains 2 minutes per hour. The slow clock loses 3 minutes per hour. At a certain time, Abigail sets both clocks to the same, correct, time. Less than 24 hours later, when the fast clock says the time is 7:00 and the slow clock says the time is 6:00, what is the actual time?

2. Friday Carmela rode the bus to school. When she left her house, she walked for 9 minutes to her bus stop, where she waited 13 minutes for the bus. The bus ride to school took 27 minutes. She waited 4 minutes for school to start. School was 6 hours and 41 minutes long. After school, she waited 8 minutes for the bus and the bus ride to her bus stop took 24 minutes. From her bus stop, she walked for 13 minutes to get to her house. If Carmela left her house at 7:15 in the morning, at what time in the afternoon did she arrive back at her house?

2._____

Name: _____

Grade: _____

School: _____

SCORE: # 3 _____

SCORE: # 4 _____

Scorer's initials _____   Scorer's initials _____

DO NOT BEGIN UNTIL YOU ARE INSTRUCTED TO DO SO

The second pair of problems is on the other side of this sheet. When instructed to begin, pick up your pencil and begin working. Record your final answer in the designated space on the problem sheet. All answers must be complete, legible, and simplified to lowest terms. This round allows the use of calculators, and calculations may also be done on scratch paper, but no other aids are allowed. If you complete the problems before time is called, use the time remaining to check your answers.

Scoring: Ten points will be awarded for each correct answer. No deduction is taken for incorrect answers or skipped problems.

3. Guillermo has 36 coins consisting of nickels and quarters. The total value of his coins is $6.20. How many quarters does Guillermo have?

3._____

4. Yi-Mei has 23 shapes, which are triangles, squares or hexagons. She has at least one of each shape. She has more triangles than squares, and more squares than hexagons. Counting up all the sides of all the figures gives a total of 78 sides. What is the largest number of triangles Yi-Mei can have?

4._____

Elementary School Target Test 11021

Name: _____

Grade: _____

School: _____

SCORE: # 5 _____

SCORE: # 6 _____

Scorer's initials _____   Scorer's initials _____

DO NOT BEGIN UNTIL YOU ARE INSTRUCTED TO DO SO

The third pair of problems is on the other side of this sheet. When instructed to begin, pick up your pencil and begin working. Record your final answer in the designated space on the problem sheet. All answers must be complete, legible, and simplified to lowest terms. This round allows the use of calculators, and calculations may also be done on scratch paper, but no other aids are allowed. If you complete the problems before time is called, use the time remaining to check your answers.

Scoring: Ten points will be awarded for each correct answer. No deduction is taken for incorrect answers or skipped problems.

5. Consecutive numbers are counting numbers that follow in order, such as: 3, 4, 5, 6, 7, and so forth. Suppose the average of a set of 17 consecutive numbers is 17. What is the average of the first 7 numbers in the set?

5._____

6. DJ is a two digit number, where D and J represent different digits. A new number is formed by putting a 5 at the end of DJ. The difference between the new number and DJ is 347. What is the value of the digit represented by D?

6._____

Elementary School Target Test 11021

Name: _____

Grade: _____

School: _____

SCORE: # 7 _____

SCORE: # 8 _____

Scorer's initials _____   Scorer's initials _____

DO NOT BEGIN UNTIL YOU ARE INSTRUCTED TO DO SO

The fourth pair of problems is on the other side of this sheet. When instructed to begin, pick up your pencil and begin working. Record your final answer in the designated space on the problem sheet. All answers must be complete, legible, and simplified to lowest terms. This round allows the use of calculators, and calculations may also be done on scratch paper, but no other aids are allowed. If you complete the problems before time is called, use the time remaining to check your answers.

Scoring: Ten points will be awarded for each correct answer. No deduction is taken for incorrect answers or skipped problems.

7. Zana's swimming pool measures 12 meters by 18 meters. The pool is surrounded by a deck 3 meters wide, as in the below drawing. What the area of the deck around Zana's pool?

7.

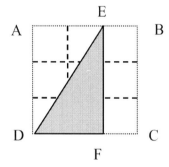

8. In the figure below, ABCD is a square which contains nine small congruent squares as shown. Point E is two-thirds of the way from A to B. Point F is two-thirds of the way from D to C. The area of triangle DEF (the shaded region) is 48 square units. What is the area of square ABCD, in square units?

8.

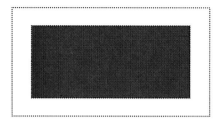

Problems 1-10

Team Name: _____
School: _____
Team Members: (Captain)_____

_____

_____

_____

SCORE: _____

Scorer's Initials: _____   Scorer's Initials: _____

DO NOT BEGIN UNTIL YOU ARE INSTRUCTED TO DO SO

This round of the competition consists of 10 problems, which the team has 20 minutes to complete. Team members may work together in any way to solve the problems. Team members may talk during this section of the competition. This round allows the use of calculators, and calculations may also be done on scratch paper, but no other aids are allowed. All answers must be complete, legible, and simplified to lowest terms. The team captain must record answers on her/his own problem sheet. If the team completes the problems before time is called, use the remaining time to check your answers.

Scoring: Ten points will be awarded for each correct answer. No deduction is taken for incorrect answers or skipped problems.

1. Charlotte wrote down all the odd numbers between 1 and 200. How many times did the digit 3 appear in Charlotte's list?

1. _____

2. N is the 5-digit number 7A65B in which A and B are digits, and N is divisible by 36. What is the smallest number N can be?

2. _____

3. What is the value of the sum of the first 100 natural numbers $(1 + 2 + 3 + 4 + ... + 100)$ minus the sum of the next 100 natural numbers $(101 + 102 + 103 + 104 + ... + 200)$?

3. _____

4. In October, Tocher convinced his parents to give him his allowance under a new system. Each day, they would give him double the amount they gave him the day before. So, on October 1 his parents gave him 1 cent. On October 2, they gave him 2 cents. On October 3, they gave him 4 cents. On October 4, they gave him 8 cents. This continued until the morning of October 12, when Tocher's parents realized that Tocher was very smart and had set up a great allowance system. How much total allowance had Tocher's parents given him from October 1 through October 11?

4.

5. Ingrid opens her book and notices that the sum of numbers of the two pages facing her is 489. What is the number of the very next page?

5. _____

6. A natural number X is greater than 10. When X is divided by 3, the remainder is 1. When X is divided by 4, the remainder is 1. When X is divided by 5, the remainder is 1. When X is divided by 6, the remainder is 1. When X is divided by 7, the remainder is 1. What is the smallest possible value of X?

6. _____

7. The cold water faucet of a bathtub can fill the tub in 12 minutes. The drain of the bathtub, when opened, can empty the full tub in 15 minutes. Suppose the tub is empty, the drain is open, and the cold water faucet is turned on. How long, in minutes, does it take to fill the bathtub?

7. _____

8. In the numbers ABCD and EFGH, different letters represent different digits, and neither of the digits A or E can be zero. If EFGH is subtracted from ABCD, what is the largest possible result?

8. _____

9. Arjun made a purchase for D dollars and C cents, and gave the cashier a $20 bill. The cashier incorrectly charged Arjun C dollars and D cents, and returned $6.85 in change. If the cashier had charged Arjun the correct price, what would the correct change have been?

9. _____

10. Jemaine and Bret have each taken 5 math contests. The score on each math contest was a whole number. Jemaine's average score on the five contests is 81.2, and Bret's average score is 86.8. If Bret scores 74 on the sixth math contest, what is the smallest possible score Jemaine can get on the sixth math contest so that he has a higher average score on the first six math contests than Bret?

10. _____

Sprint Test

1. B. 2015
2. D. Wednesday
3. C. $6.30
4. B. 394
5. A. 1233
6. D. 3
7. A. $1.05
8. C. 55
9. D. 10
10. A. 27
11. B. octagon
12. D. 245
13. C. 5
14. A. 33
15. C. 35
16. B. 17
17. D. 6/14
18. B. 122
19. A. 200
20. C. 12 sq cm
21. D. $3.96
22. A. 82188531
23. D. 20
24. C. $0.72
25. B. 3013
26. C. 32
27. D. 2
28. A. 144
29. C. $39.75
30. B. 36

Target Test

1. 6:36
2. 3:34
3. 22 (quarters)
4. 18 (triangles)
5. 12
6. 3
7. 216 (square meters)
8. 144 (square units)

Team Test

1. 30
2. 73656
3. -10,000
4. $40.95
5. 246
6. 421
7. 60 (minutes)
8. 8853
9. $4.87
10. 103

Sprint Test Solutions

1. If this year is Ava's 10th birthday, her 16th birthday will be in 6 more years. 2009 + 6 = 2015. **Answer: 2015 (B)**

2. A week is 7 days. 165 days ÷ 7 days in a week gives 21 weeks with 4 days left over. 4 days after Saturday is Wednesday. **Answer: Wednesday (D)**

3. One day of kangaroo food costs (2 x $0.45) = $0.90. One week costs (7 x $0.90) = $6.30. Tie me kangaroo down, sport!. **Answer: $6.30 (C)**

4. 90 + 300 + 4 = 394. The values were put out of order to try to confuse you! **Answer: 394 (B)**

5. We could divide all four numbers by 9 and see which one doesn't have a remainder, but there's a faster way! A number is divisible by 9 if and only if the sum of its digits is divisible by 9. The sums of the digits of the four answers are 9, 10, 12, and 15, respectively. The only number the sum whose digits is divisible by 9 is 1233. **Answer: 1233 (A)**

6. The smallest value for the sum of two prime numbers is 2 + 2 = 4. Since 3 is less than 4, it can not be the sum of two prime numbers. (To check, 14 = 3 + 11, 13 = 2 + 11, 7 = 2 + 5). **Answer: 3 (D)**

7. Pei-Chan had (1 x 25) + (2 x 10) + (5 x 5) + (4 x 1) = 64 cents. His mother gave him (3 x 10) + (1 x 1) + (2 x 5) = 41 cents. His total is 64 + 41 = 105 cents, or $1.05. **Answer: $1.05 (A)**

8. We could add up all the numbers in the parenthesis and then take one-third, but there's a faster way. Notice that each number is a multiple of 3. By the distributive property, we can take one-third of each number and then add them together. We get (1 + 2 + 3 + 4 + ... + 10) = 55. **Answer: 55 (C)**

9. Let's work backwards with the ratios. Since 21 = (3 x 7), 21 Noogies is worth (3 x 5) = 15 Boogies. Since 15 = (5 x 3), 15 Boogies is worth (5 x 2) = 10 Oogies. **Answer: 10 (D)**

10. We could multiply together (12 x 12 x 12), then multiply together (4 x 4 x 4), then divide, but there's a faster way. Since 12 = (3 x 4), we can rewrite (12 x 12 x 12) as (3 x 4 x 3 x 4 x 3 x 4) = (3 x 3 x 3) x (4 x 4 x 4). When we divide by (4 x 4 x 4), the (4 x 4 x 4) terms cancel out and we're left with (3 x 3 x 3) = 27. **Answer: 27 (A)**

11. A hexagon has 6 sides. An octagon has 8 sides. A pentagon has 5 sides. A rectangle has 4 sides. The octagon has the most sides. **Answer: octagon (B)**

12. Since one week is seven days, one week and three days is 10 days. 10 days x 24 hours in a day = 240 hours. Add the other five hours and we get 245 hours. **Answer: 245 (D)**

13. (9876 ÷ 5) has remainder 1 (since 6 ÷ 5 has remainder 1). (1234 ÷ 10) has remainder 4 (since it ends in 4). 1 + 4 = 5. **Answer: 5 (C)**

14. The sum of the digits of 2009 = (2 + 0 + 0 + 9) = 11. The sum of the digits of 2010 = (2 + 0 + 1 + 0) = 3. 11 x 3 = 33. **Answer: 33 (A)**

15. We can do this using area. The area of the brownie pan is (10 x 14) = 140 square inches. One little brownie is 4 square inches. This means the big brownie made (140 ÷ 4 =) 35 little brownies. **Answer: 35 (C)**

16. Let's work through this carefully. If Evelyn is 6 this year, then 2 years ago she was 4. Then, this year, Teresa is (4 + 10) = 14. In three years, Teresa will be (14 + 3) = 17. **Answer: 17 (B)**

17. We could find the common multiple of 8, 10, 12, and 14 and convert all the fractions, but that's a lot of work. Notice that the value of each numerator is one less than half the value of the denominator. For example, if we added 1 to the 6 in 6/14, we'd get 7/14 which is 1/2. So the 6/14 is 1/14 less than 1/2. Doing this for all four fractions means we can figure out how far away each fraction is from 1/2 (how much we'd subtract from 1/2 to get that fraction). Respectively, those values are 1/8, 1/10, 1/12, and 1/14. 1/14 is the smallest, and this means that 6/14 is the biggest of the fractions (since it's closest to 1/2). **Answer: 6/14 (D)**

18. July and January have 31 days each, November and June have 30 days each. 31 + 31 + 30 + 30 = 122. **Answer: 122 (B)**

19. We could add up all those numbers, but that's sure a lot of work and we might make a mistake. Instead, notice that if we pair up the bigger and smaller numbers, we can make pairs that add up to 25. (20 + 5), (19 + 6), (18 + 7), etc, down to

(12 + 13). There are 8 pairs total, so the sum of the numbers is (8 x 25) = 200. **Answer: 200 (A)**

20. If the squares are joined to form the rectangle, then the area of the rectangle must be the same as the combined area of all the squares. A square with perimeter 8 has side length (8/4 =) 2 and area (2 x 2 =) 4. There are three squares so their combined area is (3 x 4 = 12). **Answer: 12 (C)**

21. If Jorge and Mateo split the cost equally, then they each bought 1 sandwich, 2 cookies, and 1 lemonade. So they each spent $1.99 + (2 x $0.49) + $0.99 = $1.99 + $0.98 + $0.99 = $3.96 **Answer: $3.96 (D)**

22. What? Multiply those two numbers by hand? No way! First, look at the answers. Notice that they are the same except for the value of the tens' digit! Since the answer is one of the four answers, we only have to figure out the value of the tens' digit. We can do this by figuring out the tens' digit of (53 x 27). (53 x 27) = 14931, the tens' digit is 3, and the answer must be 82188531. **Answer: 82188531 (A)**

23. If the three digit palindrome number is less than 300, it must start with 1 or 2. So it must be of the form 1D1 or 2D2 where D can be any digit from 0 to 9. Since there are 10 digits, there are 10 numbers of the form 1D1 (101, 111, etc) and 10 numbers of the form 2D2 (202, 212, etc). So there are 20 numbers total. **Answer: 20 (D).**

24. Since she has at least one coin, 4 of her 7 coins are already determined (1 penny, 1 nickel, 1 dime, 1 quarter). There are 3 coins left that can be anything. The largest amount of money the 3 coins would be is if they were all quarters, and that would be 75 cents ($0.75). The smallest amount of money the 3 coins would be is if they were all pennies, and that would be 3 cents ($0.03). The difference is (75 - 3 =) 72 cents, or $0.72. **Answer: $0.72 (C)**

25. Wow, that's a lot of numbers. Doing the math in order would take forever. But look at the pattern, and we can rewrite it as 2009 + (2008 - 2007) + (2006 - 2005) + ... + (4 - 3) + (2 - 1). Each of the pairs of numbers have a difference of 1, and there are (2008/2 =) 1004 pairs. So the answer is 2009 + 1004 = 3013. **Answer: 3013 (B).**

26. This is a great problem for working backwards. Don had 4 marbles after he gave half to Peggy,

so before he gave marbles to Peggy he must have had 8 marbles (4 to Peggy and he kept 4). Similarly, before he gave marbles to Joan he must have had 16, and before he gave marbles to Betty he must have had 32. So he started with 32 marbles. (To check our answer, start with Don having 32 marbles and walk through the problem.) **Answer: 32 (C).**

27. Oh no, that's a huge multiplication! But let's think about it another way. From problem #22 on this test, we can assume that to find the hundreds' digit, we would only need to multiply together the parts of the numbers starting with the hundreds' place (999 x 777). But that's still pretty hard. Now, notice that 999 = (1000 - 1). So, (999 x 777) = (1000 - 1) x 777 = (1000 x 777) - (1 x 777) = 777000 - 777 = 776223. The hundreds' digit of (999 x 777) is 2, so the hundreds' digit of the original giant multiplication is also 2. **Answer: 2 (D).**

28. To make the largest possible sum, each number must be as large as possible. They are each less than 50, and each different, so the largest numbers they can be are 49, 48, and 47. (49 + 48 + 47) = 144. **Answer: 144 (A)**

29. First let's figure out the final cost of 10 cookies, which is (10 x $1.75) - $2.00 = $17.50 - $2.00 = $15.50. Joon buys 25 cookies, which is 10 cookies plus 10 cookies plus 5 cookies. So his final cost is $15.50 + $15.50 + ($1.75 x 5) = $15.50 + $15.50 + $8.75 = $39.75. **Answer: $39.75 (C)**

30. We could write down every number where the ones' digit is larger than the tens' digit, but that would take a while. Let's look at parts of the problem and see if we can find a pattern. If the ones' digit is 9, then the tens' digit could be anything from 1 to 8 (19, 29, 39, ... 89). There are 8 such numbers. If the ones' digit is 2, the tens' digit could be anything from 3 to 9. There are 7 such numbers. If the ones' digit is 3, the tens' digit could be 4 through 9. There are 6 such numbers. See the pattern? When we follow it to the end, we see that when the ones' digit is 8, there's only 1 number, (which is 98). Adding up the count, we get that the number of two digit numbers with a ones' digit larger than the tens' digit is 8 + 7 + 6 + 5 + 4 + 3 + 2 + 1 = 36. **Answer: 36 (B)**

Target Test Solutions

1. If the fast clock gains 2 minutes per hour, and the slow clock loses 3 minutes per hour, then one hour after they were set to the same, correct, time, the times they showed would be (2 + 3 =) 5 minutes apart. Since the clocks are now an hour apart, and an hour is 60 minutes, the clocks were set to the same, correct, time (60 / 5 =) 12 hours ago. In those 12 hours, the slow clock has lost (12 x 3 =) 36 minutes. So the correct time is 6:00 + 36 minutes = 6:36. (We can check this by noting that the fast clock has gained 12 x 2 = 24 minutes and taking 24 minutes from 7:00). **Answer: 6:36**

2. For this one, we convert everything to minutes and be very careful when we add them up. All of the time are already in minutes except for the length of the school day. School was 6 hours and 41 minutes, which is (6 x 60) + 41 = 360 + 41 = 401 minutes. The total number of minutes for Carmela's whole day is (9 + 13 + 27 + 4 + 401 + 8 + 24 + 13) = 499 minutes. 499 minutes is 8 hours and 19 minutes. Carmela left her house at 7:15, and 8 hours and 19 minutes after 7:15 is 3:34 in the afternoon. **Answer: 3:34**

3. If Guillermo's coins were all nickels, their value would be (36 x 5 =) 180 cents, or $1.80. Since this is less than $6.20, some of the nickels must be replaced by quarters. To have the value of his coins be $6.20, he must increase the value by ($6.20 - $1.80) = $4.40. Each nickel that is replaced by a quarter increases the value of his coins by (25 - 5 =) 20 cents. Since (440 / 20) = 22, he must have replaced 22 nickels by quarters and he must have (36 - 22 =) 14 nickels and 22 quarters. Let's check: (22 x 25) + (14 x 5) = 550 + 70 = 620 cents = $6.20. **Answer: 22 (quarters)**

4. Since she has at least one triangle, one square and one hexagon, there are 20 shapes left which can be any of the three. But she has to have more squares than hexagons, so she must have at least 2 squares. That leaves 19 shapes. If we make them all triangles, then she has 20 triangles, 2 squares, and 1 hexagon That's 74 sides total, which isn't enough. We can trade triangles for squares or hexagons, but we have to make sure she has more squares than hexagons. Trade 1 triangle for a square, and we're at 19 triangles, 3 squares, 1 hexagon, and 75 sides total. Trade 1 more triangle for a hexagon and it's 18 triangles, 3 squares, 2 hexagons. That's 78 sides total, and

so the most triangles Yi-Mei can have is 18 triangles. **Answer: 18 (triangles)**

5. This is a pretty big problem, so let's first see if we can solve a smaller problem and learn something about the average of consecutive numbers. Take the first 5 consecutive numbers (1, 2, 3, 4, 5). Their sum is 15 and their average is 3, which is the middle number. Try the 7 consecutive numbers starting with 3, which are (3, 4, 5, 6, 7, 8, 9). Their sum is 42 and their average is 7, which is the middle number. In fact, it's true that in a set of consecutive numbers that contains an odd number of consecutive numbers, the average is always the middle number. With this information, we can solve the problem. In a set of 17 consecutive numbers whose average is 17, the middle number is 17. This means that there are 8 consecutive numbers before 17. Those numbers are 9, 10, 11, 12, 13, 14, 15, 16. The first seven of these numbers are 9, 10, 11, 12, 13, 14, 15, and their average will be the middle number 12. You could also do a "guess and check" approach with this problem by guessing that the first number in the set was 1, then figuring out the average of the first 17 numbers (which is 9) and adjusting your guess until you figure out that the first number of the set must be 9. **Answer: 12**

6. The new number can be represented as DJ5 and their difference can be represented as (DJ5 - DJ). Since this value is 347, we have that DJ5 - DJ = 347. This means that J must be 8. We now have (D85 - D8 = 347). D must be 3 and the original number was 38. We can check by making sure that (385 - 38) = 347, which is true. **Answer: 3**

7. One way to approach this problem is to take the area of the deck around the pool and divide it up into squares and rectangles. By extending the lines of the sides of the pool out, we end up with 4 squares that have side length 3, two rectangles that have sides 12 and 3, and two rectangles that have sides 18 and 3. The area of all these together is (4 x (3 x 3)) + (2 x (12 x 3)) + (2 x (18 x 3)) = 36 + 72 + 108 = 216 (square meters) **Answer: 216 square meters**

The area of triangle AEF is one-half of the area of rectangle AEDF, and the area of rectangle AEDF is two-thirds the area of square ABCD. So the area of rectangle AEDF is 2 times the area of triangle AEF, and the area of square ABCD is 3/2 times the area of rectangle AEDF. This means that the area of rectangle AEDF is (2 x 48

=) 96 square units, and the area of square ABCD = (3/2) x 96 = (3 x 48) = 144 square units.
Answer: 144 (square units)

Team Round Solutions

1. First, let's think about all the odd numbers from 1 to 99, and realize which ones contain the digit 3. There's the odd numbers that end in 3 (3, 13, 23, 33, 43, 53, 63, 73, 83, 93) and the odd numbers that start with 3 (31, 33, 35, 37, 39). Note that 33 appears in both these lists, so if we put the lists together, we have (3, 13, 23, 31, 33, 35, 37, 39, 43, 53, 63, 73, 83, 93) The digit 3 appears 15 times in this list. For the odd numbers from 100 to 200, the list would be the same as above, but with 100 added to each number (103, 113, 123, etc). So the digit 3 appears 15 times in the odd numbers from 100 to 200. Overall, the digit 3 appears (15 + 15 =) 30 times in Charlotte's list of the odd numbers from 1 to 200. **Answer: 30**

2. If 7A65B is divisible by 36, then it must be divisible by 4 and by 9. If it's divisible by 4, then the number formed by the last two digits, which is 5B, must be divisible by 4. This is only true when B is 2 or 6. If 7A65B is divisible by 9, then the sum of the digits (7 + A + 6 + 5 + B) must be a multiple of 9. When B is 2, then A must be 7, and the number is 77652. When B is 6, then A must be 3, and the number is 73656. Of these two numbers, the second is smaller. **Answer: 73656**

3. Sure, we could add all these numbers up on our calculator and then take the difference, but then that would take all the time. Instead, notice how each term in the second sum is 100 more than a term in the first sum (101 vs 1, 102 vs 2, up to 200 vs 100). So their difference will be 100 times the number of pairs, which is also 100 (each sum has 100 terms). Since the second sum is larger than the first sum, the value of the difference will be 100 x (-100) = -10,000. **Answer: -10,000**.

4. We can figure out how much allowance Tocher's parents gave him each day (1, 2, 4, 8, 16, 32, 64, 128, 256, 512, 1024, 2048) and then add them all up, but that would take a while. Let's look at the total allowance after each day and see if we can find a pattern. After 2 days, Tocher has received (1 + 2 =) 3 cents. The next day he gets 4 cents and his total is 7 cents. The next day, he gets 8 cents and the total is 15 cents. The next day, he gets 16 cents ... hmmm ... it looks like Tocher's

total allowance is always one less than the allowance he will get the next day. Since Tocher's parents gave him 2048 cents on October 11, they would have given him 4096 cents on October 12. So his total allowance through October 11 is (4096 - 1) = 4095 cents = $40.95. **Answer: $40.95.**

5. When you open a book, the page numbers of the two pages facing you are consecutive numbers, and their sum is always one more than twice the number of the page on the left. (Try it with a book and confirm it's true!) So the number of the page on the left is one-half of (489 - 1) = one-half of 488 = 244. The number of the page on the right is 245, and the number of the very next page in the book will be 246. **Answer: 246.**

6. If X leaves a remainder of 1 when it is divided by 3, 4, 5, 6, and 7, then the number one less than X (X - 1) would be divisible by 3, 4, 5, 6, and 7. So the smallest possible value of (X - 1) would be the smallest number that is divisible by 3, 4, 5, 6, and 7 (the least common multiple of those numbers). That's a lot to figure out all at once, so let's do it in stages. The smallest number that is divisible by 3 and 4 is 12. The smallest number that is divisible by 12 and 5 is 60. The smallest number that is divisible by 60 and 6 is 60. The smallest number that is divisible by 60 and 7 is 420. So if X minus 1 is 420, then X is (420 + 1 =) 421. **Answer: 421.**

7. There's a couple of approaches we can use here. One is to find an amount of time that evenly divides both 12 and 15 and see what happens in the tub during that time. 3 divides both 12 and 15. In three minutes, the faucet can fill 3/12 = 1/4 of the tub. But the open drain can empty 3/15 = 1/5 of the tub. So, in 3 minutes, what part of the tub will be full of water? The answer is (1/4 - 1/5 =) 1/20 full. To fill the entire tub, it would take (3 * 20 =) 60 minutes. **Answer: 60 (minutes).**

8. If we want the difference (ABCD - EFGH) to be as large as possible, then ABCD should be as large as possible, and EFGH should be as small as possible. Since each letter is a different digit, the largest EFGH can be is 9876. The smallest ABCD can be, if A can not be zero, is 1023. The difference is (9876 - 1023 =) 8853. **Answer: 8853.**

9. If the cashier returned $6.85 in change from the $20 bill, then the cashier charged Arjun $13.15.

Since this was the incorrect amount, this means that C is 13 and D is 15. Switching these means that the correct price was $15.13 and the correct change from the $20 bill would have been ($20 - $15.13 =) $4.87. **Answer: $4.87**

10. If Jemaine's average after six math contests is going to be higher than Bret's average, then Jemaine's total score will have to be higher than Bret's total score. Bret's total score after the first five contests is (5 x 86.8 =) 434. Adding in his score on the sixth contest (74) means that Bret's total score after six contests is (434 + 74 =) 508. Jemaine's total score after five contests is (5 x 81.2 =) 406. So on the sixth contest Jemaine must score more than (508 - 406 =) 102 points. Since the score on a math contest is a whole number, the smallest possible score Jemaine can get to have a higher average is 103. **Answer: 103.**

Problems 1-30

Name: _____

School: _____

Grade: _____

Correct: _____

Incorrect: _____

SCORE (5 x Correct - 1 x Incorrect) = _____

Scorer's Initials: _____   Scorer's Initials: _____

DO NOT BEGIN UNTIL YOU ARE INSTRUCTED TO DO SO

This round of the competition consists of 30 problems. You will have 40 minutes to complete the problems. You are <u>NOT</u> allowed to use calculators, slide rules, books, or any other aids during this round. If you are wearing a calculator wrist watch, please put it on the end of the table now. Calculations may be done on scratch paper. Record only the letter of the answer in the blanks in the right-hand column of the competition booklet. If you complete the problems before time is called, use the remaining time to check your answers.

<u>Scoring</u>: Five points will be awarded for each correct answer. One point will be deducted for each incorrect answer. No deduction is taken for skipped problems.

1. What is the value of 1617 + 1718 + 1819?
   A) 4851   B) 5144   C) 5154   D) 5254

2. 120406 ÷ 11 =
   A) 1246   B) 10906   C) 12496   D) 10946

3. Which of the following numbers is NOT prime?
   A) 79   B) 77   C) 73   D) 71

4. 9 tens plus 3 hundreds minus 7 ones equals
   A) 383   B) 397   C) 937   D) 923

5. $\dfrac{2}{3}$ x $\dfrac{6}{5}$ x $\dfrac{10}{9}$ =

   A) $\dfrac{18}{17}$ B) $\dfrac{8}{9}$ C) $\dfrac{4}{9}$ D) $\dfrac{60}{135}$

6. 27 is what percent of 60?
   A) 30%   B) 35%   C) 45%   D) 50%

7. In the land of CoCo, 3 pocos equals 1 moco, 5 locos equals 1 joco, and 10 mocos equals 4 jocos. How many pocos equals 2 locos?
   A) 3   B) 4   C) 5   D) 10

8. What is the largest number that evenly divides both 231 and 105?
   A) 1   B) 3   C) 15   D) 21

9. At the snack bar, a soda costs 49 cents, a fruit roll-up costs 29 cents, and a granola bar costs 69 cents. How much will 2 sodas, 5 fruit roll-ups, and 3 granola bars cost?
   A) $4.60   B) $4.50   C) $4.40   D) $4.30

10. (24 x 24) - (16 x 16) =
    A) (8 x 8)   B) (40 x 40)   C) (8 x 2)   D) (8 x 40)

11. What is the remainder when (11 x 10 x 9 x 8 x 7 x 6) is divided by (1 x 2 x 3 x 4 x 5)?
    A) 11   B) 44   C) 7   D) 0

12. I takes Andre 2.5 hours to drive the 150 miles from Sacramento to Santa Cruz. What is Andre's average speed on the trip (in miles per hour)?
    A) 50   B) 55   C) 60   D) 75

1. _____

2. _____

3. _____

4. _____

5. _____

6. _____

7. _____

8. _____

9. _____

10. _____

11. _____

12. _____

13. Jin gave one-half of his candy to Jack and one-third of his candy to Kate. What fraction of his candy did Jin have left?

    A) $\dfrac{1}{3}$ B) $\dfrac{1}{6}$ C) $\dfrac{1}{18}$ D) $\dfrac{2}{9}$

    13. _____

14. Courtney has a length of string. She can make 36 squares with sides of length 2 inches. If she makes triangles with sides of length 3 inches, how many triangles can she make?
    A) 8 B) 12 C) 24 D) 32

    14. _____

15. What is the remainder when 1678394 is divided by 9?
    A) 4 B) 7 C) 2 D) 0

    15. _____

16. Which of the following fractions is the SMALLEST?

    A) $\dfrac{5}{65}$ B) $\dfrac{4}{44}$ C) $\dfrac{2}{24}$ D) $\dfrac{3}{42}$

    16. _____

17. Carem has six different positive whole numbers and their average is 18. She picks five of the six numbers and takes their average. She gets 20. What number did Carem NOT pick?
    A) 4 B) 8 C) 15 D) 16

    17. _____

18. Which of the following is the largest?
    A) (5x5) B) (4x4x4) C) (3x3x3x3) D) (2x2x2x2x2)

    18. _____

19. Zami bought a book whose cover price was $18.00. After the sales tax was added, the final amount Zami paid was $19.08. What was the sales tax rate, in percent?

    A) 6% B) $6\dfrac{2}{3}$ % C) 7.5% D) 8%

    19. _____

20. A square, an equilateral triangle, and a regular hexagon all have the same perimeter. If the area of the square is 36 sq cm, what is the length of a side of the regular hexagon?
    A) 9 cm B) 4 cm C) 8 cm D) 6 cm

    20. _____

21. 15 x 39 - 5 x 102 + 3 x 35 - 30 = ?
    A) 150 B) 0 C) 50 D) 2,070,675

    21. _____

22. What is the value of (307 x 209 x 111)?
    A) 7122013 B) 7122053 C) 7122073 D) 7122093

    22. _____

23. Kathy uses the digits 1, 3, 5 and 9 to make four-digit numbers by using each digit exactly once. What is the difference between the second-largest number she can make and second-smallest number she can make?
A) 7956   B) 8118   C) 7992   D) 8172

23. _____

24. What is the largest prime number that is less than 110?
A) 103   B) 105   C) 107   D) 109

24. _____

25. Desmond runs 5 miles at a constant speed of 11 feet per second. How long, in minutes, does it take him to run the 5 miles?
A) 40   B) 55   C) 45   D) 50

25. _____

26. Which of the following four math operations results in the LARGEST result?

A) $1\frac{4}{5} + 1\frac{2}{3}$ B) $1\frac{4}{5} - 1\frac{2}{3}$ C) $1\frac{4}{5} \times 1\frac{2}{3}$ D) $1\frac{4}{5} \div 1\frac{2}{3}$

26. _____

27. Amy, her two parents, and her two brothers go to a football game. An adult ticket is $23 and a child ticket is $16. They can also buy a family pass for $69. If Amy and her brothers are eligible to purchase child tickets, how much money does the family save by buying a family pass?
A) $16   B) $9   C) $25   D) $23

27. _____

28. Today (May 15, 2010) is a Saturday. What day of the week will May 14, 2011 fall on?
A) Friday   B) Saturday   C) Sunday   D) Monday

28. _____

29. Camille takes an odd prime number and multiplies it by itself, then adds an even number that is not negative. Which of the following can NOT be the answer?
A) 7   B) 9   C) 11   D) 29

29. _____

30. _____

30. Katie the Boxing Kangaroo hops three times for every two times she punches. At the end of her boxing match, the sum of her hops and her punches was 105. How many times did Katie hop in the boxing match?
A) 105   B) 23   C) 42   D) 63

Name: _____

Grade: _____

Team/School: _____

SCORE: # 1 _____

SCORE: # 2 _____

Scorer's initials _____   Scorer's initials _____

DO NOT BEGIN UNTIL YOU ARE INSTRUCTED TO DO SO

This round of the competition consists of eight problems. They will be presented to you in pairs. Work on one pair of the problems will be completed and answers will be collected before the next pair will be distributed. The time limit for each set of the two problems is six minutes. The first pair of problems is on the other side of this sheet. When instructed to begin, pick up your pencil and begin working. Record your final answer in the designated space on the problem sheet. All answers must be complete, legible, and simplified to lowest terms. This round allows the use of calculators, and calculations may also be done on scratch paper, but no other aids are allowed. If you complete the problems before time is called, use the time remaining to check your answers.

Scoring: Ten points will be awarded for each correct answer. No deduction is taken for incorrect answers or skipped problems.

1. Rose's family donated the entire contents of their "change jar" to charity. In the change jar were 243 pennies, 87 nickels, 49 dimes, 85 quarters, and four dollar coins. How much money was in the change jar?

1._____

2. Sawyer is racing in the Great Australian Animal Race. In this race, you run a 5 mile race (against a kangaroo), swim a 1 mile race (against a crocodile), and climb a 100 foot tree (against a koala). If Sawyer's total time for all three races is less than the animals' total time, Sawyer wins. A kangaroo runs at 4 miles per hour. A crocodile swims at 1.5 miles per hour. A koala climbs 2.5 feet per minute. Sawyer runs at a speed of 6 miles per hour, but he only swims at a speed of 0.75 miles per hour. As long as Sawyer can climb faster than a certain speed (in feet per minute), he can win the race. What is that speed?

2._____

Name: _____

Grade: _____

Team/School: _____

SCORE: # 3 _____

SCORE: # 4 _____

Scorer's initials _____   Scorer's initials _____

DO NOT BEGIN UNTIL YOU ARE INSTRUCTED TO DO SO

The second pair of problems is on the other side of this sheet. When instructed to begin, pick up your pencil and begin working. Record your final answer in the designated space on the problem sheet. All answers must be complete, legible, and simplified to lowest terms. This round allows the use of calculators, and calculations may also be done on scratch paper, but no other aids are allowed. If you complete the problems before time is called, use the time remaining to check your answers.

Scoring: Ten points will be awarded for each correct answer. No deduction is taken for incorrect answers or skipped problems.

3. Rose is going to France for a vacation and she needs French money (euros). At the airport, there is a money exchange center where she can exchange American dollars for French euros. For each one dollar she exchanges, she can receive 0.80 euros. The exchange center charges a fee for exchanging money. The fee is $7.95 for the first 100 dollars exchanged, and then 3 cents for each dollar exchanged after the first 100. If Rose wants to end up with 140 French euros, how much money (in American dollars and cents) must she give the money exchange center? (Round to the nearest cent, and an error of plus or minus 1 cent will be allowed).

3. _____

4. Sun has three squares, one with side length 6, one with side length 8, and one with side length 10. She arranges them so that the corner of the second square is at the center of the first square, and that the corner of the third square is at the center of the second square. The result is figure shown in the diagram below. What is the area of this figure?

4. _____

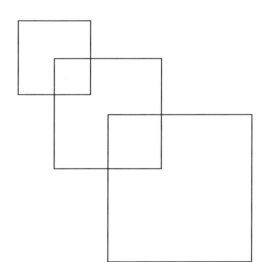

Name: _____

Grade: _____

Team/School: _____

SCORE: # 5 _____

SCORE: # 6 _____

Scorer's initials _____   Scorer's initials _____

DO NOT BEGIN UNTIL YOU ARE INSTRUCTED TO DO SO

The third pair of problems is on the other side of this sheet. When instructed to begin, pick up your pencil and begin working. Record your final answer in the designated space on the problem sheet. All answers must be complete, legible, and simplified to lowest terms. This round allows the use of calculators, and calculations may also be done on scratch paper, but no other aids are allowed. If you complete the problems before time is called, use the time remaining to check your answers.

Scoring: Ten points will be awarded for each correct answer. No deduction is taken for incorrect answers or skipped problems.

5. If the sum of the first 111 natural numbers $(1 + 2 + 3 + 4 + \ldots + 111)$ is 6216, what is the sum of the natural numbers from 9 to 119 $(9 + 10 + 11 + 12 + \ldots + 119)$?

5._____

6. A group of people is invited to a special community event. All the people are put into Room #1. Next, half of them are chosen to go to Room #2. Next, one-third of the people in Room #2 are chosen to go to Room #3. Next, 25% of the people in Room #3 are chosen to go to Room #4. Finally, 20% of the people in Room #4 are chosen to go to Room #5. At the start of the event, there were 840 people in Room #1. When the event was over, how many people were in Room #5?

6._____

Elementary School Target Test 11022

Name: _____

Grade: _____

Team/School: _____

SCORE: # 7 _____

SCORE: # 8 _____

Scorer's initials _____   Scorer's initials _____

DO NOT BEGIN UNTIL YOU ARE INSTRUCTED TO DO SO

The fourth pair of problems is on the other side of this sheet. When instructed to begin, pick up your pencil and begin working. Record your final answer in the designated space on the problem sheet. All answers must be complete, legible, and simplified to lowest terms. This round allows the use of calculators, and calculations may also be done on scratch paper, but no other aids are allowed. If you complete the problems before time is called, use the time remaining to check your answers.

Scoring: Ten points will be awarded for each correct answer. No deduction is taken for incorrect answers or skipped problems.

7. When 90 is divided by a certain number D, the remainder is 10. What is the smallest possible value of the number D?

7._____

8. Juliet is a contestant on the game show *FIND THOSE SQUARES!*. On this show, a contestant is shown a diagram and wins money for finding squares. For each square she finds, she wins money equal to the area of the square in square units. For example, for finding a 1 unit by 1 unit square she wins $1; for finding a 2 unit by 2 unit square she wins $4. Juliet is shown the below diagram. If she finds all the squares in the diagram, how much money will Juliet win?

8._____

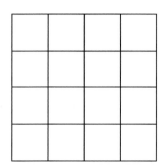

Problems 1-10

Team Name: _____

School: _____

Team Members: (Captain)_____

_____

_____

_____

SCORE: _____

Scorer's Initials: _____   Scorer's Initials: _____

DO NOT BEGIN UNTIL YOU ARE INSTRUCTED TO DO SO

This round of the competition consists of 10 problems, which the team has 20 minutes to complete. Team members may work together in any way to solve the problems. Team members may talk during this section of the competition. This round allows the use of calculators, and calculations may also be done on scratch paper, but no other aids are allowed. All answers must be complete, legible, and simplified to lowest terms. The team captain must record answers on her/his own problem sheet. If the team completes the problems before time is called, use the remaining time to check your answers.

Scoring: Ten points will be awarded for each correct answer. No deduction is taken for incorrect answers or skipped problems.

1. What is the only two-digit number whose value is equal to two times the sum of its digits?

1. _____

2. Miles adds up all the numbers from 1 through 25 (1 + 2 + 3 + ... + 24 + 25), then multiplies his sum by 26. Sawyer adds up all the numbers from 1 through 26 (1 + 2 + 3 + ... + 25 + 26), then multiplies his sum by 25. What is the positive difference between their two totals?

2. _____

3. The hot water faucet of a bathtub can fill the tub in 8 minutes. The drain of the bathtub, when opened, can empty the full tub in 10 minutes. The bathtub is half-full and the drain is closed. Michael opens the drain and turns on the how water faucet. How long (in minutes) will it take to fill the tub?

3. _____

4. Bret burps 2 times every 45 seconds. Jermaine burps once every 36 seconds. Dave burps 3 times every 50 seconds. Together, how many times do they burp in 15 minutes?

4. _____

5. 379ABC is a six-digit number where the letters A, B, and C each represent a different digit (which can not be 3, 7, or 9). If the number 379ABC is evenly divisible by 45, and the digit represented by the letter B is even, what is the largest possible value of the digit represented by the letter A?

5. _____

6. Mr. Douglas has 6 one-dollar bills that he is going to divide between his three sons Mike, Robbie, and Chip. If each son has to receive at least one dollar bill, how many different ways are there for Mr. Douglas to distribute the dollar bills between his three sons?

6. _____

7. Single copies of the new Porry Hatter book usually cost $16 each. If Libby buys 20 or more copies of the book, they cost only $13 each. How much money does Libby save by buying 20 copies of the Porry Hatter book instead of 19 copies?

7. _____

8. A rectangle is divided into two squares by a line segment going from one side to the side opposite it. If the area of one square is 25, what is the perimeter of the rectangle?

8. _____

9. The month of May has 31 days. What is the greatest number of Saturdays that could occur in the month of May?

9. _____

10. A horse and a mule are carrying packs on an expedition. The horse and the mule are each carrying a different number of sacks. The sacks are all the same size and weight. The horse says "My load is so heavy!" The mule says "Why are you complaining? If one sack was moved from your back to mine, I would be carrying twice as many sacks as you. If one sack was moved from my back to yours, we would be carrying the same number of sacks." How many sacks was the horse carrying?

10. _____

1) What is (2 + 3 + 4 + 5 - 6 - 8)? [0]

2) Today is Saturday. What day will it be 100 days from now? [Monday]

3) 36 divided by 3 equals 3 times what number? [4]

4) Sundeep and Murthy both start with the same number. Sundeep adds 6 to the number. Murthy multiplies the number by 2. They both get the same result. What number did they both start with? [6]

5) It is 2:00 PM right now. What time will it be in 100 hours? (Make sure to say if it is AM or PM). [6:00 PM]

6) Deveena has a pile of coins consisting of only quarters and dimes. Together, the change is worth 85 cents. What is the most number of dimes Deveena could have? [6]

7) What is the smallest odd prime number? [3]

8) On the math contest, a student receives 5 points for each correct answer and loses one point for each incorrect answer. Francesca gets 19 problems correct and 2 problems incorrect. What is her score? [93]

9) Karel has 8 nickels, 16 dimes, and four quarters. How much money (in dollars and cents) does he have all together? [$3.00]

10) What is the smallest positive number that can be evenly divided by 2, by 3, and by 5? [30]

11) How many dots are in the figure below? [21]

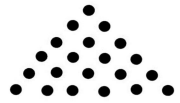

12) May 5 is a "Palindrome Day", because the number of the month and the number of the day are the same (5/5). How many Palindrome Days are there in the year 2010? [12]

13) Shen buys a robot for $5, sells it for $7, buys it back for $10, then sells it again for $16. How much profit did she make on all the deals together? [$8]

14) On the last four math contests, Yi scored 100, 84, 92 and 120. What was Yi's average score on the four math contests? [99]

15) A big cube is sliced into smaller cubes by making cuts halfway through each edge, as shown below. Once all the cuts are finished, how many smaller cubes result? [8]

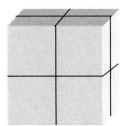

16) What is the value of 111 ones plus 1 hundred plus 11 tens? [321]

17) Greta puts the numbers starting from 1 into four columns (A, B, C, and D) using the pattern shown below. Into which column (A, B, C, or D) will Greta write the number 42? [B]

A	B	C	D
1	2	3	4
5	6	7	8
9	10	11	12

18) A digital camera and a memory card cost $100 together. If the digital camera costs $80 more than the memory card, how much does the memory card cost? [$10]

19) If a train travels 1.5 miles in one minute, what is its speed in miles per hour? [90]

20) Eloise starts with a number. She multiplies the number by 4, adds 8 to the result of that operation, then divides that result by 3. If the final result was 28, what was the original number Eloise started with? [19]

21) Perkins has floor tiles measuring 4 inches by 6 inches. How many of these tiles would take to cover a floor measuring 2 feet by 3 feet, without overlapping any tiles? [36]

22) When a number is multiplied by itself, the result is called a "square number". For example: 1 (= 1x1) and 4 (=2x2) are square numbers. What is the largest square number that is less than 100? [81]

23) VJ has 40 M&Ms, all are either red or yellow. He gives half his yellow M&Ms to Mark. After this, VJ has 27 M&Ms left. How many red M&Ms does he have? [14]

24) What is the largest multiple of 3 that is less than 100? [99]

25) What is 18 + 19 + 20 + 21 + 22? [100]

26) The product of two whole numbers is 19. What is their sum? [20]

27) 12 dozen shoes are divided into pairs. How many pairs are there? [72]

28) What is the time 7 hours and 7 minutes after 8:08 AM? (Make sure to put AM or PM after your answer) [3:15 PM]

29) If 2 groops are equal to 3 floops, and 4 floops are equal to 5 shoops, then how many groops are equal to 15 shoops? [8]

30) What is the value of (400 - 78 - 22 - 84 - 16 - 81 - 19 - 27)? [73]

31) Ana divided a certain number N by 6 and got 4 as her answer. If Carmen multiplied the same number N by 2, what would be her answer? [48]

32) Marcia is three years older than Jan. Greg is four years older than Jan. Peter is two years younger than Greg. How many years older than Peter is Marcia? [1]

33) Min has a collection of figures, all of them are either squares and triangles. She counts all the sides of the figures and gets a total of 19. What is the largest number of triangles Min could have? [5]

34) A rectangle and a square have the same area. The rectangle has side lengths of 2 and 8. What is the side length of the square? [4]

35) In one day, Sparky can eat 6 oranges and Anna can eat 2 oranges. How many days would it take the both of them to eat 24 oranges? [3]

36) What is the value of (45 + 37 + 24 - 30 - 20 - 40)? [16]

37) Rowena has a bug collection. Each day she adds 3 new bugs to her collection. If she has 28 bugs after 4 days, how many bugs will she have after 10 days? [46]

38) What is the value of (25 x 6 x 14)? [2100]

39) A swimming pool measuring 10 meters by 20 meters is enclosed by a deck that measures 1 meter in width. What is the area of the deck (in square meters)? [64]

40) Kaia stands in a line of people. She is the 13th person, counting from the front of the line. She is the 8th person, counting from the rear of the line. How many people are in the line? [20]

41) Paper clips cost 48 cents for one dozen. How many paper clips can be bought for $1? [25]

42) If the inner square has side length 4, and the outer square has side length 6, what is the area of the shaded region? [20]

43) In the months of March and April, it only rained on every odd-numbered day. In those two months, how many days did it rain? [31]

44) 8 hours and 37 minutes is how many minutes? [517]

45) There are 4 people at a party. If each person shakes hands with each other person one time, then how many handshakes will happen? [6]

46) Nikolai writes down the numbers from 1 to 100. In how many different numbers does the digit 3 appear? [19]

47) What is the largest two-digit odd number with an even tens' digit? [89]

48) If Taji can run 10 kilometers in one hour, how long (in minutes) would it take her to run 500 meters? [3]

49) When Nnendi sells a short story, she gets paid 4 cents per word. If she sells a short story that is 3500 words, how much money (in dollars) does she get paid? [$140.00]

50) Jenny can mail up to 3 books in one Special Book Mailing Box. If she has 26 books to mail, how many Special Book Mailing Boxes does Jenny need? [9]

51) If (the number of sides in a triangle) is multiplied by (the number of sides in a pentagon), what is the result? [15]

52) 2 lines can intersect in at most 1 point. What is the maximum number of points in which 4 lines can intersect? [6]

53) What is the average of 9, 18 and 36? [21]

54) Eleni has 1 quarter, 2 dimes, 3 nickels and 4 pennies. How much money (in cents) does Eleni have? [64 cents]

55) A line and a circle are drawn on a piece of paper so that the line passes through the center of the circle. How many times does the line cross the circle? [2]

56) A teacher brought 32 cookies to school for her class. Every student got a cookie, and 10 students took two cookies. If ¼ of the cookies were left over, how many students are in the class? [14]

57) Annika is watching the new *Math Girl* movie in the theatre. The movie is 1 hour and 26 minutes long, and there were 9 minutes of previews before the movie. If the previews started at 2:30, what time will the movie be done? [4:05]

58) How many positive integers less than 30 are divisible by 3 or 5 but not both? [12]

59) Azza likes to kick footballs. If he kicked one football 42 yards, two footballs 44 yards each, and one football 54 yards, what was the average distance (in yards) of all four of his kicks? [46 yards]

60) Maral has 100 pennies and Charlotte has no pennies. Maral gives half her pennies to Charlotte. Charlotte then gives half her pennies back to Maral. How many pennies does Maral have when they're done? [75]

61) What is the value of (45 + 45 + 45 + 45) + (55 + 55 + 55 + 55)? [400]

62) What is the sum of the first four positive prime numbers? [17]

63) Kylie has five coins. Only one of them is a penny. What is the least amount of money (in cents) that Kylie can have? [21 cents]

64) What is the value of (27 x 27) - (13 x 13)? [560]

MATH BOWL CHAMPIONSHIP ROUND QUESTIONS

65) In the Math Bowl Championship Round, two teams compete to answer 11 questions. Only one team can get credit for answering a question correctly. What is the minimum number of questions a team must answer correctly in order to ensure they win the Math Bowl Championship Round? [6]

66) What is (18 x 25 x 22) ÷ (55 x 15)? [12]

67) June has 10 shapes which are either triangles or squares. When June counts up all the sides, the total is 34 sides. How many triangles does June have? [6]

68) Angel uses the digits 1 through 9 to make three three-digit numbers by using each digit exactly once. He then adds the three numbers together. What is the largest possible value of the sum he gets as his result? [2556]

69) What is the ones' digit of the product (79 x 79 x 79)? [9]

70) What is (the number of faces of a cube) times (the number of vertices of a cube)? [48]

71) We define the operation Ω as the average of two numbers, in other words (A Ω B) = (A+B)/2. What is 2 Ω (6 Ω 4)? [3 1/2 or 3.5]

72) Toya has 27 cent stamps and 9 cent stamps. She needs to put a total of 72 cents on a package. What is the smallest number of stamps she can use? [4]

73) Dr. Marvin Candle was born in an interesting year. The tens digit was three times the thousands digit, the hundreds digit was three times the tens digit, and the ones digit was the sum of the tens digit and the thousands digit. What year was Dr. Candle born? [1934]

74) When a certain two-digit number is divided by 7, the remainder is 5, and when it is divided by 9, the remainder is also 5. What is the smallest possible value of the number? [68]

75) In a Fibonacci sequence, each number after the second number is the sum of the previous two numbers. For example, the sequence 1, 1, 2, 3, 5 is a Fibonacci sequence. Carlos makes a Fibonacci sequence starting with two numbers A and B. The sequence starts A, B, 11, 20, 31. What is the value of A? [2]

76) How many two digit numbers are there in which the tens digit is greater than the ones digit? [45]

77) We will call 1234 a "mountain" number because each digit, reading left to right, is larger than the previous digit. What is the largest "mountain" number that is less than 10,000? [6789]

78) Morrison is counting numbers by starting at 100 and subtracting 7 each time. So, he starts out with 100, 93, 86, and continues. What is the last positive number Morrison counts? [2]

79) A rectangle has sides whose lengths are integers (whole numbers). The perimeter of the rectangle is 18. What is the largest possible value for the area of the rectangle? [20]

80) What is the value of (26 + 27 + 28 + 29 + 30 + 31 + 32 + 33 + 34)? [270]

 Elementary School Number Sense 11022

Problems 1-80

Name: _____

School: _____

Grade: _____

Correct: _____

Incorrect: _____

SCORE: (5 x Correct - 4 x Incorrect =) _____

Scorer's Initials: _____   Scorer's Initials: _____

DO NOT BEGIN UNTIL YOU ARE INSTRUCTED TO DO SO

This is a 10-minute test. There are 80 problems. Solve accurately and quickly as many as you can in the order in which they appear. **ALL PROBLEMS ARE TO BE SOLVED MENTALLY**. Make no calculations with paper and pen/pencil. Write only the answer in the space provided for each problem. Answers must be complete, legible, and simplified to lowest terms. You are not allowed to use calculators, slide rules, books, or any other aids during this round.

Every tenth problem, marked with an asterisk (*), is an estimation problem which requires approximate integer answers. Any answer to an estimation problem that is within five percent of the correct answer will be scored correct.

Scoring: Five points will be awarded for every correct answer. For every incorrect answer or skipped problem, four points will be deducted. No deduction is taken after the last problem attempted. **Erasures, mark-overs, mark-outs, and extraneous marks on the paper ARE counted as INCORRECT**.

1. 60 - 23 = _____

2. 4 + 44 + 444 = _____

3. 13 x 2 x 5 = _____

4. 108 ÷ 9 = _____

5. What digit is in the hundredths place value of 1234.5678? _____

6. (3 x 100) + (1 x 10) + (2 x 1000) = _____

7. 12 + 13 + 14 - 15 = _____

8. 2418 ÷ 6 = _____

9. What is the numerical value of CLXXVIII (Roman numerals)? _____

10. (*) Estimate the value of (678 + 203 + 449) _____

11. 123 x 11 = _____

12. Round 6789 to the nearest thousands: _____

13. 30 x 50 x 70 = _____

14. How many odd numbers are there between 6 and 25, inclusive? _____

15. 15 x 15 = _____

16. What is the remainder when 375 is divided by 9? _____

17. 5 + 7 + 9 + 11 + 13 = _____

18. 47 x 50 = _____

19. What number added to twenty-four is thirty-three? _____

20. (*) Estimate the value of (421305 ÷ 703) _____

21. What is the smallest prime number larger than 32? _____

22. What is 15% expressed as a fraction? _____

23. 117 x 25 = _____

24. 8 yards is how many feet? _____

25. 624 - 426 = _____

26. 25 + 25 ÷ 5 = _____

27. What is the largest whole number that evenly divides both 24 and 16? _____

28. 2.1 + 3.7 + 1.4 = _____

29. 16 is to 24 as 10 is to what number? _____

30. (*) Estimate the value of (401 x 352) _____

31. Write the value of .8 as a fraction _____(fraction)

32. 10.7 + 11.6 + 3.5 = _____

33. 1.2 x 0.5 = _____

34. 18 x 22 = _____

35. 3 + 33 - 333 + 3333 = _____

36. $\frac{7}{9} - \frac{1}{9} =$ _____

37. 2 quarters and 8 nickels is equal in value to how many dimes? _____

38. (15 x 15) - (14 x 14) = _____

39. How many centimeters is $6\frac{1}{4}$ meters? _____

40. (*) Estimate the value of the positive number that, when multiplied by itself, equals 12089.

    _____

41. (6 x 6 x 6) = _____

42. How many sides does a heptagon have? _____

43. If the perimeter of a square is 32 feet, what is its area? _____ (square feet)

44. If N = 4, what is the value of (6 x N - 3)? _____

45. Write the value of $(4\frac{1}{4} \times 4\frac{3}{4})$ as a mixed number: _____

46. $15 \times 38 =$ _____

47. What is 30% of 40? _____

48. What is the next term in the sequence 2, 5, 8, 11, … ? _____

49. Write the value of $5\frac{2}{3} - 4\frac{1}{2}$ as a mixed number: _____

50. (*) Estimate the value of (39 x 40 x 41): _____

51. What is the value of $(1 + 3 + 5 + 7 + 9 + 11 + 13 + 15)$? _____

52. What number, when multiplied by 6, equals 156? _____

53. If 1 quart is 32 ounces, how many ounces is 2.5 quarts? _____

54. How many prime numbers are there that are less than 30? _____

55. What is the largest number that evenly divides 36 and 63? _____

56. A square has area 25 square meters. What is its perimeter, in meters? _____

57. What is the smallest positive integer that is a multiple of 4 and 6? _____

58. $21 \div 1\frac{3}{4} =$ _____

59. What is the largest integer that evenly divides 35, 63, and 91? _____

60. (*) Estimate the value of $(1333 \times \frac{33}{10})$: _____

61. What positive number, when multiplied by itself, equals (16 x 36): _____

62. $101 \times 123 =$ _____

63. Write the value of $(\frac{4}{5} + \frac{5}{4})$ as an improper fraction: _____

64. $16 - 42 =$ _____

65. Write the value of $\frac{9}{25}$ as a decimal: _____

66. How much (in degrees) does each angle of a square measure? _____

67. 100 x 100 x 100 = _____

68. What percent of 60 is 21? _____ %

69. What number, when multiplied by 0.25, gives a result of 1? _____

70. (*) Estimate the value of (12 x 12 x 12) _____

71. A square whose sides measure 10 cm has the same area as a rectangle whose length is 5 cm

    and whose width is what? _____ (cm)

72. 20 + 21 + 23 + 26 + 30 = _____

73. (4x4x4) x (4x4) ÷ (4x4x4x4) = _____

74. (102 x 104) = _____

75. (3 - 4 + 5 - 6 + 7 - 8 + 9 - 10 + 11 - 12) = _____

76. 15% of 16 equals 8% of what number? _____

77. (5x5) - ((3x3) + (4x4)) = _____

78. ((-3) x (5)) - (2 x 4) = _____

79. (64 x 13) + (16 x 13) = _____

80. (*) Estimate the value of (321 x 123 - 2222): _____

Elementary School 11022 Answer Key

Sprint Test

1. C
2. D
3. B
4. A
5. B
6. C
7. A
8. D
9. B
10. D
11. D
12. C
13. B
14. D
15. C
16. D
17. B
18. C
19. A
20. B
21. A
22. D
23. B
24. D
25. A
26. A
27. C
28. B
29. A
30. D

Target Test

1. $36.93
2. 4
3. $185.20
4. 175
5. 7104
6. 7
7. 16
8. $104

Team Test

1. 18
2. 325
3. 20
4. 119
5. 8
6. 10
7. $44
8. 30
9. 5
10. 5

Countdown Test

1. 0
2. Monday
3. 4
4. 6
5. 6:00 PM
6. 6
7. 3
8. 93
9. $3.00
10. 30
11. 21
12. 12
13. $8.00
14. 99
15. 8
16. 321
17. B
18. $10
19. 90
20. 19
21. 36
22. 81
23. 14
24. 99
25. 100
26. 20
27. 72
28. 3:15 PM
29. 8
30. 73
31. 48
32. 1
33. 5
34. 4
35. 3
36. 16
37. 46
38. 2100
39. 64
40. 20
41. 25
42. 20
43. 31
44. 517
45. 6

46. 19
47. 89
48. 3
49. $140.00
50. 9
51. 15
52. 6
53. 21
54. 64 cents
55. 2
56. 14
57. 4:05
58. 12
59. 46 yards
60. 75
61. 400
62. 17
63. 21
64. 560

MATH BOWL CHAMPIONSHIP ROUND

65. 6
66. 12
67. 6
68. 2556
69. 9
70. 48
71. 3.5 or 3 1/2
72. 4
73. 1934
74. 68
75. 2
76. 45
77. 20
78. 2
79. 270
80. 6789

Number Sense Test

1. 37
2. 492
3. 130
4. 12
5. 6
6. 2310
7. 24
8. 403
9. 178
10. (*) [1264-1396] (1330?)
11. 1353
12. 7000
13. 105,000
14. 10
15. 225
16. 6
17. 45
18. 2350
19. 9
20. (*) [570-629] (~600)
21. 37
22. 3/20
23. 2925
24. 24
25. 198
26. 30
27. 8
28. 7.2
29. 15
30. (*) [134094-148210] (140,000?)
31. 4/5
32. 25.8
33. 0.6
34. 396
35. 3036
36. 2/3
37. 9
38. 29
39. 625
40. (*) [105-115] (~110)
41. 216
42. 7
43. 64
44. 21
45. 20 3/16

46. 570
47. 12
48. 14
49. 1 1/6
50. (*) [60762-67158] (64000?)
51. 64
52. 26
53. 80
54. 10
55. 9
56. 20
57. 12
58. 12
59. 7
60. (*) [4179-4618] (~4400)
61. 24
62. 12423
63. 41/20 = 2 1/20
64. -26
65. 0.36
66. 90
67. 1,000,000
68. 35
69. 4
70. (*) [1642-1814] (~1728)
71. 20
72. 120
73. 4
74. 10608
75. -5
76. 30
77. 0
78. -23
79. 1040
80. (*) [35398-39124] (~30,000)

For the estimation problems, the numbers in brackets are the range of acceptable values for the answer. The number in parentheses is the exact answer.

Sprint Test Solutions

1. 1617+1718+1819 = 3335 + 1819 = 5154. **Answer: 5154 (C)**

2. Dividing it gives 10946. Check: 10946 x 11 = 109460 + 10946 = 120406. **Answer: 120406 (D)**

3. 77 = 7 x 11. **Answer: 77 (B)**

4. 90 + 300 - 7 = 390 - 7 = 383. **Answer: 383 (A)**

5. The product = 120 / 135 = (8 x 15) / (9 x 15) = 8/9. **Answer: 8/9 (B)**

6. 27/60 = 9/20 = 45/100 = 45% **Answer: 45% (C)**

7. If 5 locos equals 1 joco, then 20 locos equals 4 jocos. 4 jocos also equals 10 mocos. 10 mocos equals 30 pocos. So, 20 locos equals 30 pocos, so 2 locos equals 3 pocos. **Answer: 3 (A)**

8. 231 = 21 x 11 = 3 x 7 x 11. 105 = 5 x 21 = 5 x 3 x 7. They both have (3 x 7) in common, so the largest number that equally divides both of them (also called the Greatest Common Factor) is 21. **Answer: 21 (D)**

9. We could do all the multiplication ((2 x 49) + (5 x 29) + (3 x 69)). There is a faster way. Each item costs one penny less than a multiple of 10, so we can figure out the amount as multiples of 10, then subtract one penny per item. ((2 x 50) + (5 x 30) + (3 x 70) - 10) = (100 + 150 + 210 - 10) = 450 cents = $4.50. **Answer: $4.50 (B)**

10. (24 x 24) - (16 x 16) = 576 - 256 = 320 = (8 x 40). **Answer: (8 x 40) (D)**

11. We notice that 5 divides 10, 4 divides 8, and (2x3) = 6. So the bottom evenly divides the top, and the remainder is zero. **Answer: 0 (D)**

12. Speed = Distance divided by Time. Andre's speed = 150 / 2.5 = 300 / 5 = 60 miles per hour. **Answer: 60 (C)**

13. Jin gave away (one-half plus one-third) of his candy. So he gave away (1/2 + 1/3) = (2/6 + 3/6) = 5/6 of his candy. So he had (1 - 5/6) = 1/6 of his candy left. **Answer: 1/6 (B)**

14. Each square that Courtney makes has perimeter (4 x 2) = 8 inches. So she has (8 x 36) = 288 inches of string. Each triangle would have a perimeter of (3 x 3) = 9 inches. So she can make 288/9 = 32 triangles. **Answer: 32 (D)**

15. We could divide it out, but there's a faster way. The remainder when a number is divided by 9 is equal to the remainder when (the sum of its digits) is divided by 9. So the remainder is (1 + 6 + 7 + 8 + 3 + 9 + 4)/9 = 38/9 = 4 with remainder 2. **Answer: 2 (C)**

16. Let's simplify all four fractions. They become (from A to D), 1/13, 1 11, 1/12 and 1/14. Since they have the same numerator (1), the smallest fraction is the one with the largest denominator which is 1/14 which is D. **Answer: 3/42 (D)**

17. For the six numbers, their sum is (6 x 18) = 108. Once Carem removes a number, the sum is (5 x 20) = 100. The difference is the number she removed: (108 - 100) = 8. **Answer: 8 (B)**

18. The four values are, from A to D, 25, 64, 81, and 32. The largest is 81, which is C. **Answer: (3x3x3x3) (C)**

19. The amount of sales tax is the difference between the cover price and the final amount paid, which is $19.08 - $18.00 = $1.08. To find the percentage, we divide the sales tax by the cover price. $1.08 / $18.00 = 6/100, which is 6%. **Answer: 6% (A)**

20. If the area of the square is 36, its side has length 6, and its perimeter is 24. This is also the perimeter of the hexagon. Since a hexagon has 6 sides, the side has length 24/6 = 4. **Answer: 4 (B)**

21. We could do all the multiplication and subtraction and addition, but maybe there's a faster way. (5 x 102) = (15 x 34). (3 x 35) = (15 x 5). 30 = (15 x 2). So the value becomes (15 x 39) - (15 x 34) + (15 x 7) - (15 x 2). We can factor out the 15 to get 15 x (39 - 34 + 7 - 2) = 15 x (10) = 150. **Answer: 150 (A)**

22. Look at the answers. Notice that they are the same except for the value of the tens' digit! Since the answer is one of the four answers, we only have to figure out the value of the tens' digit. We can do this by figuring out the tens' digit of the product which would be (7 x 9 x 11) = (63 x 11) = 693, the tens' digit is 9, and the answer must be 7122093. **Answer: 7122093 (D)**

23. The largest number she can make is 9531 and the second-largest is 9513. The smallest is 1359 and the second-smallest is 1395. The difference is (9513 - 1359) = 8154. **Answer: 8154 (B).**

24. 105 is not prime (105 = 5 x 21) so it's not 105. We can check each number by trying to divide it by the prime numbers that are less than 11 (since 11 x 11 is greater than each of the numbers). Since we're looking for the largest number, let's start with 109. 109 turns out to be prime. **Answer: 109 (D)**

25. 11 feet per second is (11 x 60) = 660 feet per minute. Since one mile is 5280 feet, it takes Desmond 5280/660 = 8 minutes to run one mile. Five miles takes him (5 x 8) = 40 minutes. **Answer: 40 (A).**

26. Since both numbers are greater than 1, division and subtraction both result in numbers that are less than 1 4/5, so the answer must be multiplication or addition. When we add the two fractions, we get 2 and 22/15, or 3 and 7/15. When we multiply, we get (9/5 x 5/3) = (45/15) = 3. **Answer: 1 4/5 + 1 2/3 (A).**

27. If they bought individual tickets, they would pay (2 x $23) + (3 x $16) = $46 + $48 = $94. They save $94 - $69 = $25. **Answer: $25 (C).**

28. There are 365 days in a year and 7 days in a week, so one year is 52 weeks and 1 day. This means that May 15, 2011 will be one day more than May 15, 2010. So May 15, 2011 is Sunday, which means that May 14, 2011 is Saturday. **Answer: Saturday (B)**

29. The smallest odd prime is 3, and (3 x 3) = 9. Since the smallest even number that is not negative is 0, the smallest answer is 9. So 7 can't be the result. **Answer: 7 (A)**

30. Since she hops three times for every two punches, the sum of her hops and punches will be a multiple of 5 and the hops will be 3/5 times that total. Since there were 105 (hops and punches), the number of hops is 3/5 * 105 = 315/5 = 63. **Answer: 63 (D)**

Target Test Solutions

1. The total of the money, in cents, is (243 x 1) + (87 x 5) + (49 x 10) + (85 x 25) + (3 x 100) = (243 + 435 + 490 + 2125 + 300) = 36.93. There was $36.93 in the money jar. **Answer: $36.93**

2. First, let's figure out how long it takes, in minutes, for the animals to do the three parts of the race. For the kangaroo, 5 miles at 4 miles per hour takes (5/4) = 1.25 hours, which is (1.25 x 60) = 75 minutes. For the crocodile, a 1 mile swim takes (1/1.5) = 2/3 hours, which is (2/3 x 60) = 40 minutes. For the koala, the climb takes (100/2.5) = 40 minutes. The animals' total time is (75 + 40 + 40) = 155 minutes. Now, let's do Sawyer's times. The run takes him (5/6 x 60) = 50 minutes. The swim takes him (1/0.75) = 4/3 hour, which is 80 minutes. To win, he must climb the tree in less than (155 - 50 - 80) = 25 minutes. 100 feet in 25 minutes = 4 feet per minute. **Answer: 4**

3. Rose must give the exchange center enough American dollars to pay the fee and to get 140 euros back. First, let's do the euros. Since she gets 0.80 Euros for each dollar, to get 1 Euro (= 0.80 + ¼ (0.80)) she must exchange (1 + ¼ dollars) = $1.25. To get 140 euros, she must exchange ($1.25 x 140) = $175.00. The fee for exchanging $175.00 will be $7.95 for the first 100 dollars plus (0.03 x 75) = $2.25 for the remaining 75 dollars. The total fee is $7.95 + $2.25 = $10.20. The total she must give is $175 + $10.20 = $185.20. **Answer: $185.20**

4. The area of the whole figure will be the sum of the areas of the squares minus the areas where they overlap. The areas of the squares are (6x6) + (8x8) + (10x10) = 200. If the corner of the second square is on the center of the first square, then the area where they overlap is ¼ of the area of the small square = ¼ x36 = 9. Similarly, the area where the second and third square overlap is ¼ x 64 = 16. So the area of the overall figure is (200 - 9 - 16) = 175. **Answer: 175**

5. There are a couple ways we can approach this problem. First way: There are (111 - 1 + 1 =) 111 numbers in the first sum, and (119 - 9 + 1 =) 111 numbers in the second sum. Also, each number in the second sum is 8 more than a number in the first sum (9 and 1, 10 and 2, etc). So the second sum is (111x8 =) 888 more than the first sum, making (6216 + 888 =) 7104. Another way is to realize the second sum is equal to the first sum minus (1 + 2 + 3 + 4 + 5 + 6 + 7 + 8 =) 36, plus (112 + 113 + 114 + 115 + 116 + 117 + 118 + 119 =) 924. So the answer is (6216 - 36 + 924 =) 7104 . **Answer: 7104**

6. Let's walk through this step by step. There were 840 people in Room #1. Half of them went to Room #2, so Room #2 had (1/2 x 840 =) 420 people. One third of those (1/3 x 420 =) 140 went to Room #3. 25% is also 1/4, so (140 x 1/4 =) 35 went to Room #4. Finally 20% is 1/5, and (35 x 1/5 =) 7 people went to Room #5. **Answer: 7**

7. If the remainder was 10, then the number D must be greater than 10. Also, since 90 - 10 is 80, 80 must be a multiple of the number D (D must be a factor of 80). The only numbers greater than 10 that evenly divide 80 are 16, 20, 40 and 80. The smallest of those is 16. **Answer: 16**

8. First, let's figure out how many squares of each size are in the diagram. There are 16 squares that are 1 unit by 1 unit, 9 squares that are 2 by 2, 4 that are 3 by 3, and 1 that is 4 by 4. So Ilana wins $1 for each of the first 16 (1 by 1) squares, $4 for the next 9 (2 by 2), $9 for each of the next 4 (3 by 3), and $16 for the (4 by 4). The grand total of her winnings is (16 x $1) + (9 x $4) + (4 x $9) + (1 x $16) = $16 + $36 + $36 + $16 = $104. **Answer: $104**

Team Round Solutions

1. The smallest value of the sum of the digits of a two-digit number is $(1+0=)$ 1. The largest possible value is $(9+9=)$ 18. So the two digit number must be between 10 and $(2 \times 18 =)$ 36. It must also be even. If we quickly try all even two-digit numbers between 10 and 36, the only one that works is 18 (sum of digits is 9). **Answer: 18**

2. We're certainly not going to do all the addition in this problem. We need some sort of shorthand to help us. Let's let the symbol S represent the sum of the numbers from 1 to 25 $(1 + 2 + 3 + \ldots + 25)$. Then we can write the sums as $(S \times 26)$ and $(S + 26) \times 25$. The difference is $(25 \times 26 - S)$ which, if we write it out, turns out to be S. So the difference is $(1+2+3+ \ldots +25)$. We can add these up, or pair numbers to make 26 12 times plus 13, which is 325. **Answer: 325**

3. In 1 minute, the faucet can fill 1/8 of the tub, and the drain can drain 1/10 of the tub. So, in one minute $(1/8 - 1/10 = 5/40 - 4/40 =)$ 1/40 of the tub will be filled. Since the tub is half-full, to fill the tub ½ of it must be filled. Since ½ = 20/40, it will take 20 minutes to fill the tub. **Answer: 20.**

4. 15 minutes is $(15 \times 60 =)$ 900 seconds. In those 900 seconds, Bret burps $(900/45 \times 2) = 40$ times, Jemaine burps $(900/36 \times 1 =)$ 25 times, and Dave burps $(900/50 \times 3) = 54$ times. Together they burp $(40 + 25 + 54 =)$ 119 times. **Answer: 119.**

5. If 379ABC is divisible by 45, then it is divisible by 9 and by 5. If the number is divisible by 9, then the sum of its digits $(3+7+9+A+B+C= 19+A+B+C)$ must be divisible by 9. If the number is divisible by 5, then it must end in 0 or 5 and C must be 0 or 5. Let's look at each of these two cases. If C is 0, then $(19+A+B)$ is divisible by 9, so $(A+B)$ must be 8 or 17. A can't be 9, but A could be 8 and B could be 0. If C is 5, then $(24+A+B)$ must be divisible by 9, so $(A+B)$ must be 3 or 12. In the second case, A could be 8 and B could be 4. Either way, the biggest possible value of A is 8. **Answer: 8.**

6. Since they each have to receive at least one dollar, there's only 3 dollars left to divide between them. Let's list out all the possibilities for the distribution, with each trio of numbers being the number for Mike, Robbie and Chip respectively. The possibilities are: (1,1,4), (1,4,1), (4,1,1), (1,2,3), (1,3,2), (2,1,3), (2,3,1),

(3,1,2) and (3,2,1). This makes 10 ways. **Answer: 10.**

7. If Libby buys 19 copies, it costs $(19 \times \$16 =)$ $304. If she buys 20 copies, it costs $(20 \times \$13=)$ $260. She saves $(\$304 - \$260 =)$ $44. **Answer: $44.**

8. The line segment divides the rectangle into two squares, each of area 25. This means that the side of the square is 5. The rectangle has one square side along one of its sides, and two square sides along the other side. So the dimensions of the rectangle are 5 and 10, and the perimeter is 30. **Answer: 30.**

9. The most Saturdays would happen if the first day in May is a Saturday. So the days that would be Saturdays are May 1, May 8, May 15, May 22, and May 29, making 5 Saturdays.. **Answer: 5**

10. From when the mule and the horse are carrying the same number of sacks, we can move two sacks from the horse to the mule and then the mule would be carrying twice as many packs as the horse.Once the two packs are moved, the mule would be carrying 4 more packs than the horse (for example, if they were both carrying 3, then after two were moved the mule would have 5 and the horse would have 1). Since the amount the mule carried would be twice the amount the horse carried, the difference is the amount the horse is carrying which would be 4. So the mule was carrying 8 packs after a pack was moved from the horse to the mule, and the horse was carrying 4 packs. This means that when they first started the mule was carrying $(8-1=)$ 7 packs, and the horse was carrying $(4+1=)$ 5 packs. We can also solve this by trying possible values for the packs the horse is carrying and see if we can get numbers that fit the conditions of the problem. **Answer: 5.**

Elementary School Sprint Test 11121

Problems 1-30

Name: _____

School: _____

Grade: _____

Correct: _____

Incorrect: _____

SCORE (4 x Correct - 1 x Incorrect) = _____

Scorer's Initials: _____   Scorer's Initials: _____

DO NOT BEGIN UNTIL YOU ARE INSTRUCTED TO DO SO

This round of the competition consists of 30 problems. You will have 40 minutes to complete the problems. You are <u>NOT</u> allowed to use calculators, slide rules, books, or any other aids during this round. If you are wearing a calculator wrist watch, please put it on the end of the table now. Calculations may be done on scratch paper. Record only the letter of the answer in the blanks in the right-hand column of the competition booklet. If you complete the problems before time is called, use the remaining time to check your answers.

<u>Scoring</u>: Four points will be awarded for each correct answer. One point will be deducted for each incorrect answer. No deduction is taken for skipped problems.

1. 5 tens, minus 4 ones, plus 3 tenths, minus 2 hundredths equals
   A) 46.28   B) 46.32   C) 45.68   D) 54.32

   1. _____

2. What is the value of 67 + 678 + 6789?
   A) 7334   B) 7514   C) 7534   D) 20,269

   2. _____

3. 5 x 6 x 7 x 8 = 20 times what number?
   A) 35   B) 42   C) 56   D) 84

   3. _____

4. Which of the following numbers IS prime?
   A) 75   B) 77   C) 79   D) 81

   4. _____

5. 6.5 yards equals how many inches?
   A) 19.5   B) 78   C) 216   D) 234

   5. _____

6. If 3 BaBas equals 4 LaLas, 5 LaLas equals 8 GaGas, and 1 GaGa equals 9 YaYas, how many YaYas equals 5 BaBas?
   A) 96   B) 45   C) 26   D) 15

   6. _____

7. $\frac{3}{4} \times \frac{8}{9} \times \frac{6}{7} =$

   A) $\frac{5}{7}$ B) $\frac{4}{7}$ C) $\frac{3}{7}$ D) $\frac{2}{7}$

   7. _____

8. What number is 64% of 75?
   A) 40   B) 45   C) 48   D) 50

   8. _____

9. At the State Fair, a deep-fried candy bar cost $2.59, a deep-fried peanut butter sandwich cost $4.49, and a deep-fried soda cost $1.49. Nate bought one sandwich, three sodas, and two candy bars. If he started with $20.00, how much money did he have left?
   A) $5.86   B) $5.76   C) $14.14   D) $14.24

   9. _____

10. (5 x 5) + (12 x 12) =
    A) (10 x 12)   B) (13 x 13)   C) (5 x 12)   D) (17 x 17)

    10. _____

11. $3\frac{5}{8}$ meters is how many millimeters?

    A) 362.5   B) 375   C) 3580   D) 3625

    11. _____

12. What is the smallest number that is a multiple of both 28 and 63? (In other words, what is the Least Common Multiple of 28 and 63?)
    A) 210   B) 252   C) 378   D) 196

    12. _____

13. Teji has two squares. The lengths of the sides of each square are whole numbers. The sum of their areas is 89. What is the length of the side of the larger square?
    A) 9   B) 7   C) 5   D) 8

    13. _____

14. What is the value of (301 + 303 + 305 + 307 + 309)?
    A) 1212   B) 1515   C) 1525   D) 1535

    14. _____

15. What is the remainder when 12345678 is divided by 11?
    A) 1   B) 4   C) 7   D) 8

    15. _____

16. Which of the following fractions is the LARGEST?
    A) $\dfrac{10}{15}$ B) $\dfrac{8}{10}$ C) $\dfrac{9}{12}$ D) $\dfrac{5}{6}$

    16. _____

17. How many prime numbers are there between 8 and 48?
    A) 11   B) 12   C) 13   D) 20

    17. _____

18. A parallelogram with four congruent sides is called a _____
    A) square   B) trapezoid   C) rhombus   D) rectangle

    18. _____

19. Maral bought a new football whose price, before sales tax, was $25.00. The sales tax was 7% of the price. What was the final amount Maral paid, including the sales tax?
    A) $25.07   B) $26.75   C) $27.25   D) $32.00

    19. _____

20. How many squares with side length 2 cm can be evenly fit, without overlap or leaving a gap, into a square with side length 8 cm?
    A) 4   B) 8   C) 12   D) 16

    20. _____

21. (3.96 ÷ 0.9) x 0.4 = ?
    A) 1.4256   B) 14.256   C) 1.76   D) 17.6

    21. _____

22. What is the value of (105 x 107 x 109)?
    A) 1224615   B) 1224625   C) 1224635   D) 1224645

    22. _____

23. How many two-digit positive numbers have exactly one "5" in them?
    A) 16   B) 17   C) 18   D) 19

    23. _____

24. Matty bakes two cookies, each in the shape of a rectangle. The sides of the second cookie are 30% longer than the corresponding sides of the first cookie. By what percent is the area of the second cookie larger than the area of the first cookie?
    A) 30%   B) 60%   C) 66%   D) 69%

    24. _____

25. Darina runs at a speed of 11 feet per second and walks at a speed of 4 feet per second. How much time, in minutes, does it take her to walk 1 mile then run 1 mile?
   A) 30   B) 39   C) 40   D) 52

25. _____

26. What is the value of $(\frac{1}{2} + \frac{1}{4} + \frac{1}{8} + \frac{1}{16} + \frac{1}{32})$?
   A) $\frac{61}{64}$ B) $\frac{63}{64}$ C) $\frac{31}{32}$ D) $\frac{29}{32}$

26. _____

27. Clementine has 12 quarters, 11 pennies, 13 dimes, and 24 nickles. How much money does she have in total?
   A) $5.81   B) $5.61   C) $6.41   D) $5.11

27. _____

28. Tram takes an even number, multiplies it by itself, then adds an odd prime number. What is the smallest possible number Tram can get as the result?
   A) 7   B) 9   C) 3   D) 5

28. _____

29. A password consist of four letters, and letters can not be repeated in the password. The password "WXYZ" is different from the password "WXZY". How many different passwords can be created from the letters A, B, D, E, and G?
   A) 625   B) 120   C) 60   D) 14

29. _____

30. _____

30. What is the value of (27 x 27 x 27) ÷ (3 x 3 x 3 x 3 x 3 x 3)?
   A) (9 x 9)   B) (3 x 3)   C) (9 x 9 x 9) D) (3 x 3 x 3)

Name: _____

Grade: _____

Team (School): _____

SCORE: # 1 _____

SCORE: # 2 _____

Scorer's initials _____   Scorer's initials _____

DO NOT BEGIN UNTIL YOU ARE INSTRUCTED TO DO SO

This round of the competition consists of eight problems. They will be presented to you in pairs. Work on one pair of the problems will be completed and answers will be collected before the next pair will be distributed. The time limit for each set of the two problems is six minutes. The first pair of problems is on the other side of this sheet. When instructed to begin, pick up your pencil and begin working. Record your final answer in the designated space on the problem sheet. All answers must be complete, legible, and simplified to lowest terms. This round allows the use of calculators, and calculations may also be done on scratch paper, but no other aids are allowed. If you complete the problems before time is called, use the time remaining to check your answers.

Scoring: Ten points will be awarded for each correct answer. No deduction is taken for incorrect answers or skipped problems.

1. The Saints and the Magpies played in the Australian Rules Football Grand Final. The sum of their scores in the Grand Final was 179. The difference of their scores was 23. If the Saints won the Grand Final, how many points did the Magpies score?

1._____

2. Alley Cat meows every 3 minutes. Tom Cat meows every 4 minutes. Kitty Cat meows every 10 minutes. If they all meow together at 8:00 PM, how many times before 11:15 PM the same night will *just two* of the cats meow together?

2._____

Elementary School Target Test 11121

Name: _____

Grade: _____

Team (School): _____

SCORE: # 3 _____

SCORE: # 4 _____

Scorer's initials _____   Scorer's initials _____

DO NOT BEGIN UNTIL YOU ARE INSTRUCTED TO DO SO

The second pair of problems is on the other side of this sheet. When instructed to begin, pick up your pencil and begin working. Record your final answer in the designated space on the problem sheet. All answers must be complete, legible, and simplified to lowest terms. This round allows the use of calculators, and calculations may also be done on scratch paper, but no other aids are allowed. If you complete the problems before time is called, use the time remaining to check your answers.

Scoring: Ten points will be awarded for each correct answer. No deduction is taken for incorrect answers or skipped problems.

3. The letters in **Math** and **Contest** are cycled separately as shown below and placed in a numbered vertical list. After line 1, the next line in which both **Math** and **Contest** are spelled correctly is row number N. What is the value of N?

1:	Math	Contest
2:	hMat	tContes
3:	thMa	stConte
:	:	:
N:	Math	Contest

4. Elaine's swimming pool measures 30 feet by 20 feet. It is enclosed by a concrete deck with constant width (as shown below). If the area of the concrete deck is 336 square feet, what is the width of the concrete deck (in feet)?

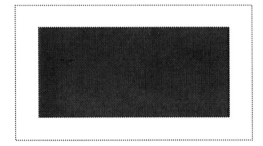

Elementary School Target Test 11121

Name: _____

Grade: _____

Team (School): _____

SCORE: # 5 _____

SCORE: # 6 _____

Scorer's initials _____   Scorer's initials _____

DO NOT BEGIN UNTIL YOU ARE INSTRUCTED TO DO SO

The third pair of problems is on the other side of this sheet. When instructed to begin, pick up your pencil and begin working. Record your final answer in the designated space on the problem sheet. All answers must be complete, legible, and simplified to lowest terms. This round allows the use of calculators, and calculations may also be done on scratch paper, but no other aids are allowed. If you complete the problems before time is called, use the time remaining to check your answers.

Scoring: Ten points will be awarded for each correct answer. No deduction is taken for incorrect answers or skipped problems.

5. Oksana likes to pick pairs of numbers and add them together. She has all the whole numbers from 1 to 2010 (1, 2, 3, …, 2009, 2010). How many *different* sums can Oksana get by picking any two of her numbers and adding them together?

5._____

6._____

6. A large rectangle is divided by two lines into four smaller rectangles, as shown below. The length of each side of each rectangle (large or small) is a whole number of inches. The areas of three of the smaller rectangles are given in the diagram below. What is the number of square inches in the total area of the original large rectangle?

6 square inches	14 square inches
15 square inches	

Elementary School Target Test 11121

Name: _____

Grade: _____

Team (School): _____

SCORE: # 7 _____

SCORE: # 8 _____

Scorer's initials _____   Scorer's initials _____

DO NOT BEGIN UNTIL YOU ARE INSTRUCTED TO DO SO

The fourth pair of problems is on the other side of this sheet. When instructed to begin, pick up your pencil and begin working. Record your final answer in the designated space on the problem sheet. All answers must be complete, legible, and simplified to lowest terms. This round allows the use of calculators, and calculations may also be done on scratch paper, but no other aids are allowed. If you complete the problems before time is called, use the time remaining to check your answers.

Scoring: Ten points will be awarded for each correct answer. No deduction is taken for incorrect answers or skipped problems.

7. How many different counting numbers will leave a
   remainder of 5 when divided into 41?

7._____

8. Space alien farmer Grbntz has a farm. On Grbntz's farm
   there are three types of creatures: Zlbns, which have three
   legs; Xyerqs, which have five legs; and Pqjkws, which have
   seven legs. One day Grbntz counts all the legs on all his
   creatures and gets 173. If Grbntz has at least two of each
   kind of creature, what is the smallest number of total
   creatures that Grbntz could have on his farm?

8._____

 Elementary School Team Test 11121

Problems 1-10

Team Name: _____

School: _____

Team Members: (Captain)_____

_____

_____

_____

SCORE: _____

Scorer's Initials: _____   Scorer's Initials: _____

DO NOT BEGIN UNTIL YOU ARE INSTRUCTED TO DO SO

This round of the competition consists of 10 problems, which the team has 20 minutes to complete. Team members may work together in any way to solve the problems. Team members may talk during this section of the competition. This round allows the use of calculators, and calculations may also be done on scratch paper, but no other aids are allowed. All answers must be complete, legible, and simplified to lowest terms. The team captain must record answers on her/his own problem sheet. If the team completes the problems before time is called, use the remaining time to check your answers.

Scoring: Ten points will be awarded for each correct answer. No deduction is taken for incorrect answers or skipped problems.

1. What is the sum of the first 2010 odd numbers?

    1. _____

2. A rectangle has a perimeter of 18 meters. The length of each of the sides of the rectangle is a whole number of meters. What is the largest possible value of the area of the rectangle, in square meters?

    2. _____

3. The cities of Dullsville, Nowheretown, and Mildburg form the points of an equilateral traingle, and each town is 120 miles from the other two towns. On Tuesday, Jared the traveling salesman drove from Dullsville to Nowheretown at 60 miles per hour, from Nowheretown to Mildburg at 40 miles per hour, and from Mildburg directly back to Dullsville at 24 miles per hour. What was Jared's average speed, in miles per hour, for his entire trip?

    3. _____

4. Azza's watch loses 6 minutes every two hours. Toby's watch gains 2 minutes every hour. At 11:00 AM Monday morning both Azza and Toby set their watches to the correct time. Later Monday, they realize that Toby's watch is exactly one hour ahead of Azza's watch. When this happens, what time is it on Toby's watch?

    4. _____

5. Fallon has four different numbers. She discovers that by adding one or more of her numbers together, she can make sums that total any whole number from 1 through 15. What are the four numbers Fallon has? [Write your answer in the form (A, B, C, D) where A, B, C, and D are the four numbers arranged from smallest to largest. For example: if the numbers were 1, 2, 3 and 4, you would write your answer as (1, 2, 3, 4).]

    5. _____

6. The rectangle below measures 3 feet by 1 foot. The two dark lines go from the midpoint of one side of the rectangle to the midpoint of a base of the rectangle. What is the area of the region between the lines (noted in the diagram), in *square inches*?

6. _____

REGION

BETWEEN THE

LINES

7. James has a bunch of triangles. Matt has a bunch of squares. Ryan has a bunch of pentagons. Brian has a bunch of hexagons. Each person has more than 1 of their type of figure. They each add up the number of sides of their figures and each end up with the same total. What is the smallest number of squares that Matt could have?

7. _____

8. How many multiples of 9 are there between 200 and 2010?

8. _____

9. "Twin primes" are two prime numbers whose difference is 2. For example, 3 and 5 are "twin primes". What is the largest pair of "twin primes" which are both less than 100? [Write your answer in the form "(A, B)" where A and B are the twin primes, with A being the smaller prime. For example, if the answer was 3 and 5 you would write (3, 5).]

9. _____

10. Bret and Jemaine are playing a game called *PICK-UP-STICK TURBO BATTLE*! In this game, players take turns picking up sticks from a pile of sticks. When it is one player's turn, that player can pick up 1, 2, 3, or 4 sticks. The winner is the last person to pick up sticks. Bret and Jemaine are starting a game, and there are 68 sticks in the pile. Bret goes first. Bret knows that if he picks up a certain number of sticks on his first turn, he can ensure he will win the game. How many sticks should Bret pick up on his first turn?

10. _____

Elementary School 11121 Answer Key

Sprint Test			Target Test	
1.	A		1.	78
2.	C		2.	22
3.	D		3.	29
4.	C		4.	3
5.	D		5.	4017
6.	A		6.	70
7.	B		7.	5
8.	C		8.	27
9.	A			
10.	B			**Team Test**
11.	D		1.	4,040,100
12.	B		2.	20
13.	D		3.	36
14.	C		4.	11:24 PM
15.	B		5.	(1, 2, 4, 8)
16.	D		6.	324 square inches
17.	A		7.	15
18.	C		8.	201
19.	B		9.	(71, 73)
20.	D		10.	3
21.	C			
22.	A			
23.	B			
24.	D			
25.	A			
26.	C			
27.	B			
28.	A			
29.	B			
30.	D			

Sprint Test Solutions

1. 50 - 4 + 0.3 - 0.02 = 46.28 **Answer: 46.28 (A)**

2. 67 + 678 + 6789 = 745 + 6789 = 7534. **Answer: 7534 (C)**

3. 5 x 6 x 7 x 8 = 5 x 6 x 7 x 2 x 4 = (5 x 4) x (6 x 7 x 2) = (20) x (84). **Answer: 84 (D)**

4. 75 = 5 x 15; 77 = 7 x 11; 81 = 9 x 9. **Answer: 79 (C)**

5. 6.5 yards (x 3 feet in a yard) = 19.5 feet. 19.5 feet x (12 inches in a foot) = 234 inches . **Answer: 236 (D)**

6. Let's convert BaBas to GaGas by finding a common amount of LaLas. Since (4x5 = 20), let's use 20 LaLas. 20 LaLas = 15 BaBas, and 20 LaLas = 32 GaGas. Since 1 GaGa = 9 YaYas, 32 GaGas = (32 x 9) = 288 YaYas and then 15 BaBas = 288 YaYas. So, 5 BaBas (= 15/3) is equal to (288/3 =) 96 YaYas . **Answer: 96 (A)**

7. 3/4 x 8/9 x 6/7 = (3x8x6)/(4x9x7) = (144/252) = (36/63) = (4/7) . **Answer: 4/7 (B)**

8. 64% of 75 = (64/100) x 75 = (16/25) x 75 = (16 x 75) / 25 = 16 x (75/25) = 16 x 3 = 48. **Answer: 48 (C)**

9. We can do all the multiplication and adding, but there's a faster way. Each item is one penny less than a multiple of ten so let's do that and subtract one penny for each item. ($4.50) + (3 x $2.60) + (2 x $1.50) - (6 x $0.01) = ($4.50 + $5.20 + $4.50) - $0.06 = $14.20 - $0.06 = $14.14. This is how much Nate spent. He started with $20.00 so he has ($20.00 - $14.14 =) $5.86 left **Answer: $5.86 (A)**

10. (5 x 5) + (12 x 12) = 25 + 144 = 169 = (13 x 13). **Answer: (13 x 13) (B)**

11. 3 5/8 meters = 3.625 meters, and 3.625 meters x (1000 millimeters in a meter) = 3625 millimeters. **Answer: 3625 (D)**

12. 28 = (2 x 2 x 7), and 63 = (7 x 3 x 3). They have 7 in common as a prime factor, so the Least Common Multiple will be (2 x 2 x 3 x 3 x 7 =) 252. **Answer: 252 (B)**

13. Since (10 x 10 =) 100 is greater than 89, the largest the side could be is 9. If the larger square has side 9, the smaller square would be a side length that, when multiplied by itself, equals 89 - (9x9) = 8. There is no whole number like that. Let's try 8. 89 - (8x8) = 89 - 64 = 25 = (5x5), so 8 is the answer. **Answer: 8 (D)**

14. The sum equals (5 x 300) + (1+3+5+7+9) = 1500 + 25 = 1525. **Answer: 1525 (C)**

15. Dividing it out, we get 12345678 = (11 x 1122334) with 4 left over. **Answer: 4 (B)**

16. Let's simplify all four fractions. They become (from A to D), 2/3, 4/5, 3/4, 5/6. Of the four, 5/6 is the largest. **Answer: 5/6 (D)**

17. Between 8 and 48, the prime numbers are: 11, 13, 17, 19, 23, 29, 31, 37, 41, 43, 47. **Answer: 11 (A)**

18. A figure with four parallel congruent sides is the definition of a rhombus. (In a square, the sides also meet at right angles). **Answer: rhombus (C)**

19. 7% of $25.00 = $1.75, so the total was $25.00 + $1.75 = $26.75. **Answer: $26.75 (B)**

20. The large square has area (8x8=) 64, the small square has area (2x2=) 4, and 64/4 = 16. Since the small squares can be put in the large square without overlap (like tiles) the answer is 16. **Answer: 16 (D)**

21. (3.96 divided by 0.9) = 4.4, and 4.4 x 0.4 = 1.76. **Answer: 1.76 (C)**

22. Look at the answers. Notice that they are the same except for the value of the tens' digit! Since the answer is one of the four answers, we only have to figure out the value of the tens' digit. Since each number is 100 plus a smaller number, we can just multiply the smaller numbers and the tens' digit of their product will be the tens' digit of the overall total. (5 x 7 x 9) = 315, so the tens' digit is 1 and 1224615 is the answer. **Answer: 1224615 (A)**

23. The two-digit numbers with <u>exactly</u> one five are 15, 25, 35, 45, 65, 75, 85, 95, the numbers from 50 through 54, and the numbers from 56, through 59. (Notice we did <u>not</u> count 55). That's (8+5+4 =) 17 numbers. **Answer: 17 (B).**

24. Since the lengths of the sides aren't specified, we can use whatever side lengths we want to make the problem simpler. Let's use 10 and 100. The first cookie has area 1000. The sides of the second cookie are (10+3=) 13, and (100+30=)130. The area of the second cookie is (13x130=) 1690. The percent increase is (1690-1000)/1000 = 690/1000 = 69/100, which is 69%. **Answer: 69% (D)**

25. 11 feet per second is (11 x 60) = 660 feet per minute. Since one mile is 5280 feet, it takes Darina 5280/660 = 8 minutes to run one mile. 4 feet per second is (4x60=) 240 feet per minute, and it takes Darina (5280/240=) 22 minutes to walk one mile. To run one mile then walk one miles takes Darina (8+22=) 30 minutes. **Answer: 30 (A).**

26. Make a common denominator, (1/2 + 1/4 + 1/8 + 1/16 + 1/32) = (16/32 + 8/32 + 4/32 + 2/32 + 1/32) = (31/32). **Answer: 31/32 (C).**

27. Adding up the money, we get (12 x $0.25) + (11 x $0.01) + (13 x $0.10) + (24 x $0.05) = ($3.00 + $0.11 + $1.30 + $1.20) = ($5.61). **Answer: $5.61 (B).**

28. Let's use the smallest possible numbers to get the smallest possible result. The smallest even number is 2, the smallest odd prime is 3, and the smallest result is (2x2) + 3 = 7. **Answer: 7 (A)**

29. There are five letters. We could use any of the five for the first letter, then any of the four remaining for the second, then any of three for the third, then any of two for the fourth. To get the asnwer, we multiply those together. (5 x 4 x 3 x 2) = 120. **Answer: 120 (B)**

30. (3 x 3 x 3 x 3 x 3 x 3) = (27 x 27), and (27 x 27 x 27) divided by (27 x 27) = 27 = (3 x 3 x 3). **Answer: (3 x 3 x 3) (D)**

Target Test Solutions

1. If we add up the values of the sum of two numbers and the difference of two numbers, the result is twice the larger number. (Try it with any two numbers and confirm for yourself that this is the case). Since $179+23 = 202 = 2 \times 101$, the larger score is 101. Since the Saints won, they scored 101 and the Magpies scored ($179 - 101 =$) 78 points. **Answer: 78**

2. First, lets figure out how long it will be until the three cats meow together again. That number will be the Least Common Multiple of 3, 4, and 10, which is 60. So, every hour the cats meow together. What happens in that hour? Alley Cat and Tom Cat meow together every 12 minutes, so just those two meow together 4 times (at 12, 24, 36, and 48 minutes after the hour). Just Tom Cat and Kitty Cat meow together every 20 minutes, at 20 and 40 minutes after the hour. Just Alley Cat and Kitty Cat meow together every 30 minutes, at 30 minutes after. In one hour, just two cats meow together 7 times. There are 3 hours from 8PM to 11PM, so in those three hours just 2 cats meow together 21 times. In the last fifteen minutes, only Alley Cat and Tom Cat meow together (at 11:12). So the answer is ($21+1=$) 22 times. Making a chart of meowing times would be a very nice way to solve this problem. **Answer: 22.**

3. "Math" is four letters long, so every four rows it will be spelled correctly. Similarly, "Contest" will be spelled correctly every 7 rows. The LCM of 4 and 7 is 28, so 28 rows later they both will be spelled correctly. 28 rows after Row 1 is Row 29, so N is 29. **Answer: 29**

4. We can cut the concrete deck into four rectangles and four squares. If W is the width of the deck, two rectangles measure 20 by W, and two measure 30 by W. The four squares measure W by W. Let's try values of W and see if they can work. If W is 1, the area of the deck is ($2 \times 30 \times 1$) + ($2 \times 20 \times 1$) + ($4 \times 1 \times 1$) = 104. If W is 2, the area is 256. If W is 3, the area is 336 and the width of the deck is 3 feet. **Answer: 3**

5. The smallest sum she can make is $0+1 = 1$. The largest sum she can make is $2009+2010 = 4019$. She can also make any sum in between 1 and 4019 by adding the two numbers that are on either side (lesser, greater) as the sum. For example, if she wants to make a sum of 3472, she can use ($3472/2 -1=$) 1735 and ($3472/2 + 1$ =) 1737. So she can get all sums between 1 and 4019.. **Answer: 4019**

6. The smallest rectangle can either be (1 x 6) or (2 x 3). It can't be (1 x 6) because the side of length 6 would be shared with either the rectangle of area 14 or the rectangle of area 15 and in either case that would mean the other side of the second rectangle wasn't a whole number (14/6 or 15/6). So the small rectangle must be (2 x 3). Also, the side of length 2 must be shared with the rectangle of area 14 and the other side of that rectangle must be 6. The side of length 3 must be shared with the rectangle of area 15 and the other side must be 5. So the big rectangle has side lengths 5 and 7 and its area is (5x7=) 35. So the whole large rectangle is size (6+14+15+35) = 70 square inches. **Answer: 70**

7. If a number leaves a remainder of 5 when divided into 41, then the number must evenly divide (41-5=) 36. So the number must be a factor of 36. The factors of 36 are: 1, 2, 3, 4, 6, 9, 12, 18, and 36. If the number leaves a remainder of 5, it must be bigger than 5. The only factors of 36 that are bigger than 5 are 6, 9, 12, 18, and 36. That's five different counting numbers, so the answer is 5. **Answer: 5**

8. Let's account for the legs of the creatures that we know Grbntz must have. If he has at least two of each creature, then the legs on two of each creature account for (2x3) + (2x5) + (2x7) = 30 legs. That leaves 143 legs left over. To have the smallest number of total creatures, we want to have mostly creatures with the most legs (the Pqjkws). Dividing 143 by 7 gives 20 Pqjkws with 3 legs left over. Since there is a 3-legged creature (the Zlbn), 143 legs could be 20 Pqjkws and 1 Zlbn. Adding the two creatures of each kind makes for a total of (21 + 1 + 6=) 27 creatures. **Answer: 27**

Team Round Solutions

1. We could try to add all the numbers up with a calculator, but that would take forever. Let's try smaller problems and look for a pattern. The sum of the first two odd numbers is 1+3=4. The sum of the first three odd numbers is 1+3+5 = 9. The sum of the first four odd numbers is 1+3+5+7 = 16. It sure looks like the sum of the first N odd numbers is NxN. (It turns out this is true, and you can prove it using algebra). So the sum of the first 2010 odd numbers is (2010 x 2010 =) 4,040,100. **Answer: 4,040,100.**

2. If the perimeter is 18 meters, the sum of the length and width is 9 and the sides could be (1,8), (2,7), (3,6), or (4,5). If the rectangle's area is going to be as large as possible, then the sides should be as close to equal as possible. So the sides should be 4 and 5 and the area would be 20 **Answer: 20**

3. On the first leg of his trip, Jared takes 2 hours. On the second leg, he takes 3 hours, and the third leg takes 5 hours. His total travel time is 10 hours, and his total distance is (3 x 120 =) 360. So his average speed is 360/10 = 36 miles per hour. **Answer: 36.**

4. The first thing we have to do is figure out how long it takes until their watches are an hour apart. If Azza's watch loses 6 minutes every 2 hours, then it loses 3 minutes every hour. Since Toby's watch gains 2 minutes every hour, after one hour they are 5 minutes apart. For the watches to be one hour apart, it will take (60/5 =) 12 hours. When the watches are one hour apart, the real time will be 11:00 PM. In those 12 hours, Toby's watch will have gained (12 x 2 =) 24 minutes. So the time on Toby's watch is 11:24 PM. **Answer: 11:24 PM.**

5. Let's walk through the sums and figure our Fallon's numbers. She can make 1 and 2, so she has to have 1 and 2. 3 = 1+2, but to make 4 she must have 4. She can make 5, 6, and 7 with 1, 2, and 4, but she must have 8. Now she can make all numbers from 9 to 15 with 1, 2, 4, 8 so those are her four numbers **Answer: (1, 2, 4, 8).**

6. If we take the triangular areas that aren't in the region and put then together, we will get a rectangle. The area of the region between the lines will be the area of the whole rectangle minus the area of the small rectangle. Let's convert everything to inches. The big rectangle is 36 inches by 12 inches. The small rectangle is 18 inches by 6 inches. The area of the region is (36x12)-(18x6) = 432- 108 = 324 square inches. **Answer: 324.**

7. If the number of sides each has is the same, it must be a number that is divisible by 3, 4, 5 and 6. The smallest number divisible by all four numbers is 60. Since they each have 60 sides, Matt must have (60/4=) 15 squares. **Answer: 15.**

8. Let's find the number of multiples of 9 between 1 and each number, and then take the difference. The number of multiples of 9 between 1 and 2010 is (2010/9=) 223. The number of multiples of 9 between 1 and 200 is (200/9=) 22. The difference is (223 - 22 =) 201. **Answer: 201.**

9. The prime numbers between 1 and 100 are: 2, 3, 5, 7, 11, 13, 17, 19, 23, 29, 31, 37, 41, 43, 47, 51, 53, 59, 61, 67, 71, 73, 79, 83, 89, 97. The largest two whose difference is 2 is 71 and 73. **Answer: (71, 73).**

10. Let's work backwards and think about how Bret would win the game. He would have to go last, which would mean when it is his turn the pile has to have 1, 2, 3, or 4 sticks. How does he make sure the pile has 1, 2, 3, or 4 sticks? Since Jemaine could pick, 1, 2, 3, or 4 sticks on his turn (before Bret), when it's Jemaine's turn there must be some number of sticks such that no matter how many Jemaine picks, Bret is left with 1, 2, 3, or 4 sticks. Notice that (1+4) = (2+3) = (3+2) = (4+1) = 5. If there were 5 sticks in the pile before Jemaine's turn, no matter how many Jemaine picked, Bret could win. From here Bret can continue to work backwards with multiples of 5. This is Bret's strategy. He must make sure that at the end of his turn, the number of sticks is a multiple of 5. Then, however many sticks Jemaine picks, Bret picks a number that makes the next multiple of five. If Jemaine picks 1 stick, Bret picks 4, etc. Since Bret is going first, he wants to pick enough sticks from the pile so that a multiple of 5 is left. Since 68-3=65, Bret should pick up 3 sticks. **Answer: 3.**

Elementary School Sprint Test 11122

Problems 1-30

Name: _____

School: _____

Grade: _____

Correct: _____

Incorrect: _____

SCORE (4 x Correct - 1 x Incorrect) = _____

Scorer's initials: _____   Scorer's initials: _____

DO NOT BEGIN UNTIL YOU ARE INSTRUCTED TO DO SO

This round of the competition consists of 30 problems. You will have 40 minutes to complete the problems. You are <u>NOT</u> allowed to use calculators, slide rules, books, or any other aids during this round. If you are wearing a calculator wrist watch, please put it on the end of the table now. Calculations may be done on scratch paper. Record only the letter of the answer in the blanks in the right-hand column of the competition booklet. If you complete the problems before time is called, use the remaining time to check your answers.

<u>Scoring</u>: Four points will be awarded for each correct answer. One point will be deducted for each incorrect answer. No deduction is taken for skipped problems.

1. Which of the following numbers is composite?
   A) 13   B) 15   C) 17   D) 19   E) Other

   1. _____

2. What is the value of 12×18?
   A) 210   B) 216   C) 222   D) 228   E) Other

   2. _____

3. How many feet are in 9 yards?
   A) 3   B) 4.5   C) 18   D) 27   E) Other

   3. _____

4. There are 100 balls in a jar. One-half of them are blue. How many of the balls are blue?
   A) 10   B) 25   C) 50   D) 100   E) Other

   4. _____

5. What is $\frac{3}{4} \times \frac{4}{5} \times \frac{5}{6} \times \frac{6}{7}$?
   A) $\frac{1}{4}$ B) $\frac{2}{5}$ C) $\frac{3}{7}$ D) $\frac{5}{9}$ E) Other

   5. _____

6. The difference of two prime numbers is 95. What is their sum?
   A) 37   B) 39   C) 91   D) 93   E) Other

   6. _____

7. Jonathan buys a $7.35 movie ticket. If he pays with a $10 bill, how much change does he receive?
   A) $2.45   B) $2.55   C) $2.65   D) $2.75   E) Other

   7. _____

8. A jacket has a regular price of $70. If the price is discounted 30% and a $10 discount is applied after that, then what is the new price in dollars?
   A) 30   B) 39   C) 49   D) 60   E) Other

   8. _____

9. What is the value of $998 + 999 + 1000 + 1001 + 1002$?
   A) 4998   B) 5000   C) 5002   D) 5004   E) Other

   9. _____

10. Aaron can cut a stick into 6 pieces in 30 seconds. If he cuts at a constant rate, then how many seconds does it take him to cut the stick into 12 pieces?
    A) 30   B) 33   C) 60   D) 66   E) Other

    10. _____

11. Mr. Carlson wins $18 million to be paid in 300 equal payments. How many dollars are in each payment?
    A) 6×10^4 B) 6×10^5 C) 6×10^6 D) 6×10^7 E) Other

    11. _____

Elementary School Sprint Test - 11122 © 2010 mathleague.org

12. Lucy invests $5000 at an annual interest rate of 6%. How many dollars does she have after one year?
    A) 4,700   B) 5,000   C) 5,300   D) 5,600   E) Other

13. Albert, Anthony, and Alex stand in a row. In how many orders can they stand?
    A) 2   B) 4   C) 5   D) 6   E) Other

14. A list of numbers is formed by starting with two numbers. The next number in the list is the product of the previous two numbers. If the fourth number is 27 and the fifth number is 81, then what is the first number?
    A) $\frac{1}{9}$ B) $\frac{1}{3}$ C) 1   D) 9   E) Other

15. What is the value of $46 \times 47 \times 48$?
    A) 103756   B) 103766   C) 103776   D) 103786   E) Other

16. Jerry is 3 years old and his mother is 31 years old. In how many years will Jerry's mother be three times as old as Jerry?
    A) 7   B) 8   C) 9   D) 10   E) Other

17. It takes 1 hen 2 days to lay an egg. In how many days will 3 hens lay 6 eggs?
    A) 3   B) 4   C) 6   D) 9   E) Other

18. 13 boys pay the same whole-dollar amount of money for a field trip. The sum of their payments is $24_, where the blank space is a digit. What is the missing digit?
    A) 5   B) 6   C) 7   D) 8   E) Other

19. In a family, each child has at least 3 brothers and 1 sister. What is the minimum number of children in the family?
    A) 3   B) 4   C) 5   D) 6   E) Other

20. Dennis is supposed to multiply a number by 4. Instead, he divides by 4 and gets 3 as his answer. What is the correct answer?
    A) $\frac{3}{4}$ B) 3   C) 12   D) 48   E) Other

21. Adam, Berta, and Carlos buy an $8 raffle ticket together. Adam pays $1, Berta pays $2, and Carlos pays $5. They win 1000 dollars and split the winnings proportionally to their contributions. How many dollars did Carlos win?
    A) 125   B) 500   C) 625   D) 750   E) Other

22. What is the largest odd factor of 7992?
    A) 333   B) 999   C) 1999   D) 3999   E) Other

22. _____

23. John writes consecutive integers starting from 5 until he has written 29 digits. What is the last digit he writes?
    A) 1   B) 2   C) 3   D) 4   E) Other

23. _____

24. Alan, Brandon, Courtney, Diana, Edward, and Frank need to split into two groups of three each. If the order of the groups does not matter (e.g. groups of [Alan, Brandon, Courtney] and [Diana, Edward, Frank] is considered the same as [Edward, Diana, Frank] and [Courtney, Brandon, Alan]), then in how many ways can they divide into groups?
    A) 3   B) 6   C) 10   D) 20   E) Other

24. _____

25. The sum of the digits of a positive two-digit number equals $\frac{1}{7}$ of the number. If the digits of the number are inverted, the number is decreased by 45. How many such numbers exist?
    A) 0   B) 1   C) 2   D) 4   E) Other

25. _____

26. The day after the day before yesterday is Thursday. What day of the week is today?
    A) Monday   B) Tuesday   C) Wednesday   D) Thursday   E) Other

26. _____

27. Nick counts the number of positive multiples of 3 less than 100. How many does he count?
    A) 30   B) 31   C) 32   D) 33   E) Other

27. _____

28. What is the least positive integer divisible by 2, 3, 4, and 5?
    A) 1   B) 6   C) 60   D) 120   E) Other

28. _____

29. Two hundred socks, each colored green, blue, red, brown, black, or white, are in a drawer. How many socks must be taken from the drawer to ensure that at least two socks of the same color have been picked?
    A) 6   B) 7   C) 193   D) 194   E) Other

30. _____

30. The number 111...1, where there are 2010 1's, is divided by 3. What is the number of zeroes in the quotient?
    A) 335   B) 669   C) 670   D) 2009   E) Other

29. _____

mathleague.org

Elementary School Target Test 11122

Name: _____

Grade: _____

Team (School): _____

SCORE: # 1 _____

SCORE: # 2 _____

Scorer's initials _____   Scorer's initials _____

DO NOT BEGIN UNTIL YOU ARE INSTRUCTED TO DO SO

This round of the competition consists of eight problems. They will be presented to you in pairs. Work on one pair of the problems will be completed and answers will be collected before the next pair will be distributed. The time limit for each set of the two problems is six minutes. The first pair of problems is on the other side of this sheet. When instructed to begin, pick up your pencil and begin working. Record your final answer in the designated space on the problem sheet. All answers must be complete, legible, and simplified to lowest terms. This round allows the use of calculators, and calculations may also be done on scratch paper, but no other aids are allowed. If you complete the problems before time is called, use the time remaining to check your answers.

Scoring: Ten points will be awarded for each correct answer. No deduction is taken for incorrect answers or skipped problems.

1. The area of a square is 100 square inches. If the side length is increased by 1 inch, then what is the new area?

1. _____

2. In how many ways can Richard make change for $1 using only nickels and dimes?

2. _____

Elementary School Target Test - 11122 © 2010 mathleague.org

Elementary School Target Test 11122

Name: _____

Grade: _____

Team (School): _____

SCORE: # 3 _____

SCORE: # 4 _____

Scorer's initials _____   Scorer's initials _____

DO NOT BEGIN UNTIL YOU ARE INSTRUCTED TO DO SO

The second pair of problems is on the other side of this sheet. When instructed to begin, pick up your pencil and begin working. Record your final answer in the designated space on the problem sheet. All answers must be complete, legible, and simplified to lowest terms. This round allows the use of calculators, and calculations may also be done on scratch paper, but no other aids are allowed. If you complete the problems before time is called, use the time remaining to check your answers.

Scoring: Ten points will be awarded for each correct answer. No deduction is taken for incorrect answers or skipped problems.

3. What is the value of the sum $1 + 3 + 5 + 7 + \cdots + 199$?

3. _____

4. 187569 consists of all different digits. What is the next integer that consists of all different digits?

4. _____

Elementary School Target Test - 11122 © 2010 mathleague.org

Elementary School Target Test 11122

Name: _____

Grade: _____

Team (School): _____

SCORE: # 5 _____

SCORE: # 6 _____

Scorer's initials _____   Scorer's initials _____

DO NOT BEGIN UNTIL YOU ARE INSTRUCTED TO DO SO

The third pair of problems is on the other side of this sheet. When instructed to begin, pick up your pencil and begin working. Record your final answer in the designated space on the problem sheet. All answers must be complete, legible, and simplified to lowest terms. This round allows the use of calculators, and calculations may also be done on scratch paper, but no other aids are allowed. If you complete the problems before time is called, use the time remaining to check your answers.

Scoring: Ten points will be awarded for each correct answer. No deduction is taken for incorrect answers or skipped problems.

5. 20 students average a score of 70 on a test, while 5 other students average a score of 80. What is the overall average of the 25 students?

5. _____

6. The diameter of a circle is 30. By what value must the radius be decreased by to decrease the area by 104π?

6. _____

Elementary School Target Test 11122

Name: _____

Grade: _____

Team (School): _____

SCORE: # 7 _____

SCORE: # 8 _____

Scorer's initials _____   Scorer's initials _____

DO NOT BEGIN UNTIL YOU ARE INSTRUCTED TO DO SO

The fourth pair of problems is on the other side of this sheet. When instructed to begin, pick up your pencil and begin working. Record your final answer in the designated space on the problem sheet. All answers must be complete, legible, and simplified to lowest terms. This round allows the use of calculators, and calculations may also be done on scratch paper, but no other aids are allowed. If you complete the problems before time is called, use the time remaining to check your answers.

Scoring: Ten points will be awarded for each correct answer. No deduction is taken for incorrect answers or skipped problems.

7. The area of a circle is equal to the side length of a square. If the radius of the circle is 1, then what is the area of the square? Express your answer as a decimal to the nearest tenth.

8. On Kush, most years have 10 months of 12 days each. Once every 6 years, a year consists of 121 days (the first month has 13 days). A week on Kush is 6 days long (the days of the week are One, Two, Three, Four, Five and Six). If Piyush was born on Six, the third day of the second month of a year with 121 days, then what day of the week was Piyush's 20th birthday?

Elementary School Target Test - 11122 © 2010 mathleague.org

Problems 1-10

Team Name: _____

School: _____

Team Members: (Captain) _____

_____

_____

_____

SCORE: _____

Scorer's Initials: _____   Scorer's Initials: _____

DO NOT BEGIN UNTIL YOU ARE INSTRUCTED TO DO SO

This round of the competition consists of 10 problems, which the team has 20 minutes to complete. Team members may work together in any way to solve the problems. Team members may talk during this section of the competition. This round allows the use of calculators, and calculations may also be done on scratch paper, but no other aids are allowed. All answers must be complete, legible, and simplified to lowest terms. The team captain must record answers on her/his own problem sheet. If the team completes the problems before time is called, use the remaining time to check your answers. Scoring: Ten points will be awarded for each correct answer. No deduction is taken for incorrect answers or skipped problems.

1. An amusement park charges an entry fee of $10.00 and $1.30 per ticket. If Courtney spends a total of $21.70, then how many tickets did she buy?

1. _____

2. The base of a triangle measures 6 units and the area is 18 square units. What is the length of the height to the base?

2. _____

3. What is the arithmetic mean of the first 10 prime numbers? Express your answer as a common fraction.

3. _____

4. Three distinct circles and two distinct lines lie in the same plane. What is the maximum number of intersection points between these 5 shapes?

4. _____

5. A rectangle has side lengths 5 and 20. Its area is equal to the area of a square. What is the side length of this square?

5. _____

6. How many integers from 1 to 300 have units digit 3 and are divisible by 3?

6. _____

7. A fair coin is flipped 12 times. What is the most likely number of heads that are flipped?

7. _____

8. Daniel rolls a red die, a green die, and a blue die. In how many ways can the sum of the number of dots on the top face be 12?

8. _____

9. What is the units digit of the number $2009 \times 2009 \times 2009 \times \cdots \times 2009$, where there are 2011 2009's?

9. _____

10. Some (at least 2) students sit at a circular table. Tony takes a bag with 400 pieces of candy, and takes a piece out. He passes the bag to his left. Each subsequent person takes one piece of candy and then passes the bag to the left. If Tony gets the last piece of candy, then how many possible values are there for the number of students at the table?

10. _____

 Elementary School Team Test - 11122 © 2010 mathleague.org

Elementary School 11122 Answer Key

Sprint Test

1. B
2. B
3. D
4. C
5. C
6. E
7. C
8. B
9. B
10. D
11. A
12. C
13. D
14. B
15. C
16. E
17. B
18. C
19. D
20. D
21. C
22. B
23. A
24. C
25. A
26. E
27. D
28. C
29. B
30. B

Target Test

1. 121
2. 11
3. 10000
4. 187590
5. 72
6. 4
7. 9.9
8. Three

Team Test

1. 9
2. 6
3. $\dfrac{129}{10}$
4. 19
5. 10
6. 10
7. 6
8. 25
9. 9
10. 7

Sprint Test Solutions

1. $15 = 3 \times 5$ so 15 is composite. **Answer: 15 (B)**

2. $12 \times 18 = 216$. **Answer: 216 (B)**

3. 3 feet are in 1 yard, so $9 \times 3 = 27$ feet are in 9 yards. **Answer: 27 (D)**

4. $\frac{1}{2} \times 100 = 50$. **Answer: 50 (C)**

5. $\frac{3}{\cancel{4}} \times \frac{\cancel{4}}{\cancel{5}} \times \frac{\cancel{5}}{\cancel{6}} \times \frac{\cancel{6}}{7} = \frac{3}{7}$. **Answer: $\frac{3}{7}$ (C)**

6. If the difference of two integers is odd, then one of them must be even. 2 is the only even prime number, so one of the numbers must be 2. It follows that the other number is 97, so the sum is 99. **Answer: 99 (E)**

7. $10 - 7.35 = 2.65$. **Answer: $2.65 (C)**

8. After the 30% discount, the price is $(1 - 0.30) \times 70 = 49$ dollars. After the $10 discount, the price is $49 - 10 = \$39$. **Answer: 39 (B)**

9. $998 + 999 + 1000 + 1001 + 1002 = (998 + 1002) + (999 + 1001) + 1000 = 2000 + 2000 + 1000 = 5000$. **Answer: 5000 (B)**

10. Aaron makes $6 - 1 = 5$ cuts in 30 seconds, so he makes 1 cut in 6 seconds. To cut the stick into 12 pieces, he makes 11 cuts, so it takes $6 \times 11 = 66$ seconds. **Answer: 66 (D)**

11. He wins 18×10^6 dollars in 3×10^2 payments. Dividing these two yields $\frac{18}{3} \times 10^{6-2} = 6 \times 10^4$ dollars per payment. **Answer: 6×10^4 (A)**

12. The interest earned is 6% of $5000, or $5000 \times 0.006 = \$300$. So the total amount is $5000 + 300 = \$5300$. **Answer: 5300 (C)**

13. Let the positions they stand in be labeled A, B, and C. There are 3 ways to choose the person who stands in position A. After choosing that, there are 2 ways to choose the person who stands in position B. The remaining person must stand in position C. So there are $3 \times 2 \times 1 = 6$ orders. **Answer: 6 (D)**

14. The product of the third and fourth numbers equals the fifth number, so the third number equals the quotient of the fifth and fourth numbers, or $\frac{81}{27} = 3$. Similarly, the second number is $\frac{27}{3} = 9$, and the first number is $\frac{3}{9} = \frac{1}{3}$. **Answer: $\frac{1}{3}$ (B)**

15. $46 \times 47 = 2162$ so $46 \times 47 \times 48 = 2162 \times 48 = 103776$. **Answer: 103776 (C)**

16. Jerry's mother is 28 years older than Jerry. So Jerry is 14 years old when Jerry's mother is three times as old as him, or $14 - 3 = 11$ years from now. **Answer: 11 (E)**

17. If 1 hen takes 2 days to lay 1 egg, then 3 hens take 2 days to lay 3 eggs. So in 4 days, 3 hens will lay 6 eggs. **Answer: 4 (B)**

18. $\frac{24\_}{13}$ must be an integer because the boys pay a whole-dollar amount. The only multiple of 13 between 240 and 249, inclusive, is 247. **Answer: 7 (C)**

19. Each girl must have at least 1 sister, so there are at least 2 girls in the family. Each boy must have at least 3 brothers, so there are at least 4 boys in the family. So the minimum is $2 + 4 = 6$ children. **Answer: 6 (D)**

20. His original number is $4 \times 3 = 12$. The number he was supposed to get is thus $12 \times 4 = 48$. **Answer: 48 (D)**

21. Carlos should win $\frac{5}{8}$ of the winnings, or $1000 \times \frac{5}{8} = 625$. **Answer: 625 (C)**

22. $7992 = 8000 - 8 = 8(1000 - 1) = 8 \times 999$. **Answer: 999 (B)**

23. First, John writes 5, 6, 7, 8, and 9, a total of 5 digits. So there are 24 digits used in the two-digit numbers that he writes. 20 digits are used from 10 to 19, so he has 4 digits left. So the last 4 digits he writes are 2, 0, 2, 1. **Answer: 1 (A)**

24. We pick Alan's group; the other group will be the rest of the people. There are $5 \times 4 = 20$ ways to pick the members of Alan's group, but this counts each group exactly twice because [Brandon, Courtney] is counted as well as [Courtney, Brandon] and similarly for the rest of them. So there are $\frac{20}{2} = 10$ ways to choose the groups. **Answer: 10 (C)**

25. The number must be divisible by 7, so the possibilities for the number are: 14, 21, 28, 35, 42, 49, 56, 63, 70, 77, 84, 91, and 98. The first criterion leaves the possible numbers to be 21, 42, 63, or 84. Checking, none of these numbers are decreased by 45 upon inversion of digits. **Answer: 0 (A)**

26. The day before yesterday is Wednesday, so today is Friday. **Answer: Friday (E)**

27. Every third number from 1 to 99 is divisible by 3. 100 is not divisible by 3, so the answer is $\frac{99}{3} = 33$. **Answer: 33 (D)**

28. The number must be divisible by 2, 3, $4 = 2 \times 2$, and 5. Hence, the least positive integer divisible by these four number is $3 \times 4 \times 5 = 60$. **Answer: 60 (C)**

29. For any group of 7 socks, the socks cannot be all of different colors. But for a group of 6 socks, they can all be different colors. **Answer: 7 (B)**

30. Note that $\frac{111}{3} = 37$, $\frac{111111}{3} = 37037$, $\frac{111111111}{3} = 37037037$. So $\frac{111\ldots1}{3} = 37037037\ldots037$, where 037 is repeated 669 times. Thus, there are a total of 669 zeroes in the quotient. **Answer: 669 (B)**

Target Test Solutions

1. The original side length of the square is $\sqrt{100} = 10$. So the new side length is $10 + 1 = 11$, and the new area is $11 \times 11 = 121$ square inches. **Answer: 121**

2. If the number of dimes is between 0 and 10 inclusive, then there is an amount of nickels that satisfies the problem. But if there are 11 or more dimes, then the total amount of change is greater than \$1. So the answer is $10 - 0 + 1 = 11$. **Answer: 11**

3. This is the sum of the first 100 odd numbers. By the formula for the sum of the first n odd numbers, the answer is $100 \times 100 = 10000$. **Answer: 10000**

4. The numbers from 187570 through 187579 have at least two 7's. The numbers from 187580 through 187589 have at least two 8's. Hence, the next integer that consists of all different digits is 187590. **Answer: 187590**

5. The sum of the first 20 students' scores is $20 \times 70 = 1400$ while the sum of the other 5 students' scores is $5 \times 80 = 400$. So the overall average is $\dfrac{1400 + 400}{25} = 72$. **Answer: 72**

6. The radius of the circle is 15, so the original area of the circle is $15 \times 15 \times \pi = 225\pi$. The area is decreased by 104π, so the new area is $225\pi - 104\pi = 121\pi$, and the new radius is 11. Thus, the radius is decreased by $15 - 11 = 4$ units. **Answer: 4**

7. The area of the circle is $1 \times 1 \times \pi = \pi$, so the area of the square is $\pi \times \pi \approx 9.9$. **Answer: 9.9**

8. 17 years of 120 days and 3 years of 121 days pass during Piyush's 20 years. So there are $17 \times 120 + 3 \times 121 = 2403$ days since Piyush is born, or $400 \times 6 + 3$. Hence, the day of the week has 'increased' by 3, so Piyush's 20th birthday is Three. **Answer: Three**

Team Test Solutions

1. Courtney spends $21.70 - $10.00 = $11.70 on tickets, so she buys $\dfrac{11.70}{1.30} = 9$ tickets. **Answer: 9**

2. The area is $\dfrac{1}{2}$ of the product of the base and height, so the height is two times the quotient of the area and base, or $2 \times \dfrac{18}{6} = 6$. **Answer: 6**

3. The mean is $\dfrac{2+3+5+7+11+13+17+19+23+29}{10} = \dfrac{129}{10}$. **Answer:** $\dfrac{129}{10}$

4. Two distinct circles intersect in a maximum of two points. Three distinct circles form 3 pairs of two distinct circles, forming a maximum of $3 \times 2 = 6$ intersection points. Two lines intersect in a maximum of 1 point. Finally, a line and a circle intersect in a maximum of two points. There are 6 pairs of one line and one circle, forming up to $6 \times 2 = 12$ intersection points. So the maximum number of total intersection points is $6 + 1 + 12 = 19$. **Answer: 19**

5. The area of the rectangle is $5 \times 20 = 100$, so the side length of the square is $\sqrt{100} = 10$. **Answer: 10**

6. The numbers that satisfy the condition are $3, 33, 63, \ldots, 273$; essentially every 30th number from 3 through 273. Thus, there are $\dfrac{273 - 3}{30} + 1 = 10$ such numbers. **Answer: 10**

7. The number of ways to flip $0, 1, 2, \ldots, 12$ heads are $\binom{12}{0}, \binom{12}{1}, \binom{12}{2}, \ldots, \binom{12}{12}$. $\binom{12}{6}$ is the largest of these, so the most likely number of heads is 6. **Answer: 6**

8. The possible distributions of dots are: $(6, 5, 1)$, $(6, 4, 2)$, $(6, 3, 3)$, $(5, 5, 2)$, $(5, 4, 3)$, and $(4, 4, 4)$. There are 6, 6, 3, 3, 6, and 1 ways to achieve these, respectively, so there are $6 + 6 + 3 + 3 + 6 + 1 = 25$ ways. **Answer: 25**

9. When there is 1 iteration of 2009, the units digit is 9. When there are 2 iterations of 2009, the units digit is 1. When there are 3 iterations of 2009, the units digit is 9. When there are 4 iterations, the units digit is 1. In general, if the number of iterations is odd, then the units digit is 9. **Answer: 9**

10. Tony gets one more piece than everyone else. If we disregard the piece, then everyone has the same amount of candy. Hence, the number of people at the table must be a factor of $400 - 1 = 399 = 3 \times 7 \times 19$. There are 8 such factors, but one of them is 1, which should not be counted. **Answer: 7**

Elementary School Sprint Test 11123

Problems 1-30

Name: _____

School: _____

Grade: _____

Correct: _____

Incorrect: _____

SCORE (4 x Correct - 1 x Incorrect) = _____

Scorer's initials: _____   Scorer's initials: _____

DO NOT BEGIN UNTIL YOU ARE INSTRUCTED TO DO SO

This round of the competition consists of 30 problems. You will have 40 minutes to complete the problems. You are <u>NOT</u> allowed to use calculators, slide rules, books, or any other aids during this round. If you are wearing a calculator wrist watch, please put it on the end of the table now. Calculations may be done on scratch paper. Record only the letter of the answer in the blanks in the right-hand column of the competition booklet. If you complete the problems before time is called, use the remaining time to check your answers.

<u>Scoring</u>: Four points will be awarded for each correct answer. One point will be deducted for each incorrect answer. No deduction is taken for skipped problems.

1. How many of the numbers in the list 61, 63, 65, 67, 69 are prime?
   A) 0   B) 1   C) 2   D) 3   E) Other

   1. _____

2. Evaluate $615 + 384$.
   A) 231   B) 999   C) 1000   D) 1001   E) Other

   2. _____

3. A square has side length 4. What is its area in square units?
   A) 2   B) 4   C) 8   D) 32   E) Other

   3. _____

4. The songs on Adam's iMod have length 4:15, 5:21, and 5:24. What is the average length of his songs in minutes?
   A) 3   B) 4   C) 5   D) 6   E) Other

   4. _____

5. Evaluate: $1234 \times 4321 - 4321 \times 1234$.
   A) -5332114 B) 0   C) 1   D) 5332114   E) Other

   5. _____

6. The distance from Alphonse's house to Beryl's house is 3 miles. If Alphonse bikes at a speed of 12 miles per hour, then how many minutes does it take him to bike from his house to hers?
   A) 5   B) 10   C) 12   D) 15   E) Other

   6. _____

7. Max has 3 quarters, 2 dimes, and 1 penny. How many cents does he have in total?
   A) 6   B) 92   C) 96   D) 98   E) Other

   7. _____

8. Evaluate: $\sqrt{\sqrt{16}}$.
   A) 1   B) 2   C) 4   D) 256   E) Other

   8. _____

9. The probability that it rains today is $\frac{3}{10}$ and the probability that Mrs. Halladay assigns homework is $\frac{5}{7}$. If these events are independent then what is the probability that it rains today and homework is assigned?
   A) $\frac{1}{12}$ B) $\frac{2}{13}$ C) $\frac{3}{14}$ D) $\frac{4}{15}$ E) Other

   9. _____

10. Max writes the integers from 1 through 22. How many digits does he write?
    A) 30   B) 32   C) 34   D) 36   E) Other

    10. _____

11. Courtney made 9 out of 12 free throws in a basketball game. What percent of her free throws did she make?
    A) 25   B) 50   C) 60   D) 75   E) Other

    11. _____

12. What is the next number in the sequence $1, 4, 9, 16, \_\_\_$?

    A) 19   B) 22   C) 25   D) 28   E) Other

12. _____

13. Mount Everest has a peak height of 29029 feet. If Johnny climbs up Everest on a path that travels exactly 6 feet per 1 foot elevation gain, then how many miles, to the nearest mile, does he travel if there are 5280 feet in one mile?

    A) 33   B) 36   C) 39   D) 42   E) Other

13. _____

14. What is the sum of the first 17 positive odd integers?

    A) 289   B) 291   C) 293   D) 297   E) Other

14. _____

15. How many integers between 1 and 40 are divisible by 3?

    A) 10   B) 11   C) 12   D) 13   E) Other

15. _____

16. Express five hundred thousand squared in scientific notation.

    A) 2.5×10^{11} B) 2.5×10^{12} C) 25×10^{10} D) 25×10^{11} E) Other

16. _____

17. What is 4! expressed in decimal notation?

    A) 6   B) 12   C) 24   D) 36   E) Other

17. _____

18. What is the value of 198×202?

    A) 400   B) 39996   C) 40000   D) 40004   E) Other

18. _____

19. $\frac{11}{10}$ of an integer is another integer. If the second integer is between 70 and 80, then what is the value of the first integer?

    A) 77   B) 80   C) 88   D) 90   E) Other

19. _____

20. Two angles of a triangle measure $63°$ and $79°$. What is the degree measure of the third angle?

    A) 38   B) 39   C) 48   D) 49   E) Other

20. _____

21. Convert $77°$ Fahrenheit to Celsius, given that $0°$ Celsius is $32°$ Fahrenheit and $100°$ Celsius is $212°$ Fahrenheit.

    A) 20   B) 25   C) 30   D) 35   E) Other

21. _____

22. Rick calculates all possible products of two elements from the set $\{-5, -4, -3, \ldots, 2, 3, 4\}$. What is the smallest product that he calculates?

    A) -25   B) -20   C) -15   D) 0   E) Other

22. _____

23. $2 \times 2 \times \cdots \times 2 = 64$. How many 2's are in the left side of the equation?   23. _____
   A) 3   B) 4   C) 5   D) 6   E) Other

24. The number $265d$ is divisible by 7, where d is a digit. What is the value of d?   24. _____
   A) 4   B) 5   C) 6   D) 7   E) Other

25. How many distinct ways are there to arrange the letters in START?   25. _____
   A) 20   B) 60   C) 90   D) 120   E) Other

26. How many positive integers are divisors of 20?   26. _____
   A) 2   B) 4   C) 6   D) 8   E) Other

27. In Jerry's class, 12 students own a dog, 15 students own cats, and 10 students own   27. _____
   both. 3 students own neither a cat nor a dog. How many students are in Jerry's
   class?
   A) 20   B) 21   C) 22   D) 23   E) Other

28. The sum of the radii of two circles is 12. If A is the sum of their areas, then what   28. _____
   is the smallest possible value of A?
   A) 36π B) 144π C) 288π D) 324π E) Other

29. The product of the digits of 2011 is $2 \times 0 \times 1 \times 1 = 0$. For how many of the next   29. _____
   100 integers (2012 through 2111) is the product of the digits equal to 0?
   A) 19   B) 20   C) 21   D) 22   E) Other

30. Jeffrey is a mirror salesman. For every 10 houses he visits, he sells 3 mirrors. If   30. _____
   he needs to sell 1029 mirrors each week, then how many houses must he visit each
   week?
   A) 3430   B) 3520   C) 3610   D) 3700   E) Other

Elementary School Target Test 11123

Name: _____

Grade: _____

Team (School): _____

SCORE: # 1 _____

SCORE: # 2 _____

Scorer's initials _____   Scorer's initials _____

DO NOT BEGIN UNTIL YOU ARE INSTRUCTED TO DO SO

This round of the competition consists of eight problems. They will be presented to you in pairs. Work on one pair of the problems will be completed and answers will be collected before the next pair will be distributed. The time limit for each set of the two problems is six minutes. The first pair of problems is on the other side of this sheet. When instructed to begin, pick up your pencil and begin working. Record your final answer in the designated space on the problem sheet. All answers must be complete, legible, and simplified to lowest terms. This round allows the use of calculators, and calculations may also be done on scratch paper, but no other aids are allowed. If you complete the problems before time is called, use the time remaining to check your answers.

Scoring: Ten points will be awarded for each correct answer. No deduction is taken for incorrect answers or skipped problems.

1. A pyramid has base area 12 square inches and height 4 inches. What is its volume in cubic inches?

   1. _____

2. Alphonse, Beryl, Carly, and Dan play a game. Starting with 2011 marbles, Alphonse takes away 1 marble, Beryl takes away 2 marbles, Carly takes away 3 marbles, and Dan takes away 4 marbles. Alphonse then takes away another marble, Beryl another 2, etc. Who takes the last marble?

   2. _____

Elementary School Target Test 11123

Name: _____

Grade: _____

Team (School): _____

SCORE: # 3 _____
SCORE: # 4 _____
Scorer's initials _____   Scorer's initials _____

DO NOT BEGIN UNTIL YOU ARE INSTRUCTED TO DO SO

The second pair of problems is on the other side of this sheet. When instructed to begin, pick up your pencil and begin working. Record your final answer in the designated space on the problem sheet. All answers must be complete, legible, and simplified to lowest terms. This round allows the use of calculators, and calculations may also be done on scratch paper, but no other aids are allowed. If you complete the problems before time is called, use the time remaining to check your answers.

Scoring: Ten points will be awarded for each correct answer. No deduction is taken for incorrect answers or skipped problems.

3. A weighted coin has probability $\frac{2}{3}$ of landing heads. If Max flips the coin twice, what is the probability that both flips come up heads? Express your answer as a common fraction.

3. _____

4. To make a tricycle, Lola needs 1 seat, 1 frame, 2 pedals, and 3 wheels. She has 22 seats, 18 frames, 40 pedals, and 53 wheels. What is the maximum number of tricycles she can make?

4. _____

Elementary School Target Test 11123

Name: _____

Grade: _____

Team (School): _____

SCORE: # 5 _____

SCORE: # 6 _____

Scorer's initials _____   Scorer's initials _____

DO NOT BEGIN UNTIL YOU ARE INSTRUCTED TO DO SO

The third pair of problems is on the other side of this sheet. When instructed to begin, pick up your pencil and begin working. Record your final answer in the designated space on the problem sheet. All answers must be complete, legible, and simplified to lowest terms. This round allows the use of calculators, and calculations may also be done on scratch paper, but no other aids are allowed. If you complete the problems before time is called, use the time remaining to check your answers.

Scoring: Ten points will be awarded for each correct answer. No deduction is taken for incorrect answers or skipped problems.

5. An integer is called *quasi-perfect* if the sum of its proper divisors is 1 greater than the number itself. How many numbers between 1 and 10, inclusive, are quasi-perfect?

5. _____

6. The sum of a positive integer and itself is equal to its product with itself. What is the integer?

6. _____

Elementary School Target Test 11123

Name: _____

Grade: _____

Team (School): _____

SCORE: # 7 _____

SCORE: # 8 _____

Scorer's initials _____   Scorer's initials _____

DO NOT BEGIN UNTIL YOU ARE INSTRUCTED TO DO SO

The fourth pair of problems is on the other side of this sheet. When instructed to begin, pick up your pencil and begin working. Record your final answer in the designated space on the problem sheet. All answers must be complete, legible, and simplified to lowest terms. This round allows the use of calculators, and calculations may also be done on scratch paper, but no other aids are allowed. If you complete the problems before time is called, use the time remaining to check your answers.

Scoring: Ten points will be awarded for each correct answer. No deduction is taken for incorrect answers or skipped problems.

7. How many vertices does a cube have? 7. _____

8. What is the area of the largest circle that can fit inside a 4×6 rectangle? Express your answer in terms of π. 8. _____

mathleague.org

Elementary School Team Test 11123

Problems 1-10

Team Name: _____

School: _____

Team Members: (Captain) _____

_____

_____

_____

SCORE: _____

Scorer's Initials: _____   Scorer's Initials: _____

DO NOT BEGIN UNTIL YOU ARE INSTRUCTED TO DO SO

This round of the competition consists of 10 problems, which the team has 20 minutes to complete. Team members may work together in any way to solve the problems. Team members may talk during this section of the competition. This round allows the use of calculators, and calculations may also be done on scratch paper, but no other aids are allowed. All answers must be complete, legible, and simplified to lowest terms. The team captain must record answers on her/his own problem sheet. If the team completes the problems before time is called, use the remaining time to check your answers. Scoring: Ten points will be awarded for each correct answer. No deduction is taken for incorrect answers or skipped problems.

1. Tony goes to the post office to buy stamps. If he has $23 and stamps cost 46 cents each, then how many stamps can he purchase?

1. _____

2. If 2 bloops is 1 bleep and 5 bleeps is 1 blop, then how many bloops are in 1 bloop, 1 bleep, and 1 blop?

2. _____

3. The square root of 81 is equal to the square of what positive integer?

3. _____

4. What is the sum of the first 18 positive integers?

4. _____

5. The amount of bacteria in a test tube doubles every hour. At 1:00 PM there are 50 bacteria. How many bacteria are there at 5:00 PM?

5. _____

6. The median of a set of 3 integers is 49, the mean is 51, and the range is 22. What is the value of the largest integer?

6. _____

7. John's father is 3 times as old as John. In 10 years, John's father will be 2 times as old as John. What is John's age?

7. _____

8. The square of the velocity of an object is directly proportional to its kinetic energy. If its velocity is doubled, then by what factor is its kinetic energy multiplied by?

8. _____

9. Jake knows that Chris's 4-digit locker combination consists of only odd digits. What is the maximum number of attempts (an attempt being defined as testing a number) it requires for Jake to unlock Chris's locker?

9. _____

10. Anna has a calculator. She types a positive digit (1 through 9), an operation (addition, subtraction, multiplication, or division), and another positive digit. What is the probability that her result is 4?

10. _____

Sprint

1. C
2. B
3. E
4. C
5. B
6. D
7. C
8. B
9. C
10. E
11. D
12. C
13. A
14. A
15. D
16. A
17. C
18. B
19. E
20. A
21. B
22. B
23. D
24. E
25. B

26. C
27. A
28. E
29. E
30. A

Target

1. 16
2. Alphonse
3. $\frac{4}{9}$
4. 17
5. 0
6. 2
7. 8
8. 4π

Team

1. 50
2. 13
3. 3
4. 171
5. 800
6. 63
7. 10
8. 4
9. 625
10. $\frac{13}{324}$

Sprint Round

1. Only 61 and 67 are prime. **Answer: 2 (C)**

2. $615 + 384 = 999$. **Answer: 999 (B)**

3. $4 \times 4 = 16$. **Answer: 16 (E)**

4. The sum of the times is 15 minutes, so the average is $15 \div 3 = 5$. **Answer: 5 (C)**

5. By the Commutative Property of Multiplication, $1234 \times 4321 = 4321 \times 1234$. Thus, $1234 \times 4321 - 4321 \times 1234 = 0$. **Answer: 0 (B)**

6. Alphonse takes $3 \div 12 = 0.25$ hours or $0.25 \times 60 = 15$ minutes. **Answer: 15 (D)**

7. $3 \times 25 + 2 \times 10 + 1 = 96$. **Answer: 96 (C)**

8. $\sqrt{\sqrt{16}} = \sqrt{4} = 2$. **Answer: 2 (B)**

9. $\frac{3}{10} \times \frac{5}{7} = \frac{3}{14}$. **Answer: $\frac{3}{14}$ (C)**

10. There are 9 1-digit integers and $22 - 10 + 1 = 13$ 2-digit integers. So he writes $9 \times 1 + 13 \times 2 = 35$ digits. **Answer: 35 (E)**

11. $\frac{9}{12} \times 100\% = 75\%$. **Answer: 75 (D)**

12. The numbers are the perfect squares. The next number is $5 \times 5 = 25$. **Answer: 25 (C)**

13. Johnny travels 29029×6 feet or $\frac{29029 \times 6}{5280} \approx 33$ miles. **Answer: 33 (A)**

14. The sum is $17 \times 17 = 289$. **Answer: 289 (A)**

15. The numbers are $3, 6, 9, \ldots, 39$, for $\frac{39-3}{3} + 1 = 13$. **Answer: 13 (D)**

16. $\left(5 \times 10^5\right)^2 = 25 \times 10^{10} = 2.5 \times 10^{11}$. **Answer: 2.5×10^{11} (A)**

17. $4! = 4 \times 3 \times 2 \times 1 = 24$. **Answer: 24 (C)**

18. $198 \times 202 = 200^2 - 4 = 39996$. **Answer: 39996 (B)**

19. The first integer must be divisible by 10. If it is 70, then the second integer is $\frac{11}{10} \times 70 = 77$ which works. **Answer: 70 (E)**

20. The third angle measures $180 - 63 - 79 = 38°$. **Answer: 38 (A)**

21. $\frac{5}{9}(77 - 32) = 25$. **Answer: 25 (B)**

22. The smallest possible product is $-5 \times 4 = -20$. **Answer: -20 (B)**

23. $2 \times 2 \times 2 = 8$, so $2 \times 2 \times 2 \times 2 \times 2 \times 2 = 64$. **Answer: 6 (D)**

24. 2653 is divisible by 7. **Answer: 3 (E)**

25. $\frac{5!}{2} = 60$. **Answer: 60 (B)**

26. $20 = 2^2 \times 5$, so there are $(2+1)(1+1) = 6$ divisors. **Answer: 6 (C)**

27. By the Principle of Inclusion Exclusion, the answer is $12 + 15 - 10 + 3 = 20$. **Answer: 20 (A)**

28. The smallest sum of area occurs when the radii are equal, or $r = 6$. So the answer is $36\pi + 36\pi = 72\pi$. **Answer: 72π (E)**

29. All of the integers from 2012 through 2110 have a zero, so the product of the digits will be zero. **Answer: 1 (E)**

30. He needs to visit 10 houses to sell 3 mirrors, so he needs to visit $\frac{10}{3} \times 1029 = 3430$ houses to sell 1029 mirrors. **Answer: 3430 (A)**

Target Round

1. The volume is $\frac{12 \times 4}{3} = 16$. **Answer: 16**

2. The cycle repeats every 10 marbles, so the person taking the 2011st marble is the same person who takes the 1st marble, or Alphonse. **Answer: Alphonse**

3. $\frac{2}{3} \times \frac{2}{3} = \frac{4}{9}$. **Answer: $\frac{4}{9}$**

4. She has enough seats for 22 tricycles, frames for 18 tricycles, pedals for 20 tricycles, and wheels for 17 tricycles. **Answer: 17**

5. Testing each integer from 1 through 10, we find that none of them are quasi-perfect. **Answer: 0**

6. If the integer is 1, then $1 + 1 = 1 \times 1$ which isn't true. If the integer is 2, then $2 + 2 = 2 \times 2$ which holds. **Answer: 2**

7. A cube has 8 vertices. **Answer: 8**

8. The diameter of the circle is 4 units, so the radius is 2. Hence, the area is 4π. **Answer: 4π**

Team Round

1. Tony has 2300 cents, so he can buy $\frac{2300}{46} = 50$ stamps. **Answer: 50**

2. 1 bleep is 2 bloops and 1 blop is 10 bloops, so the answer is $1 + 2 + 10 = 13$. **Answer: 13**

3. $\sqrt{81} = 9$, which is the square of 3. **Answer: 3**

4. The sum of the first 18 positive integers is $\frac{18(19)}{2} = 171$. **Answer: 171**

5. $50 \times 2 \times 2 \times 2 \times 2 = 800$. **Answer: 800**

6. The sum of the largest and smallest integers is $51 \times 3 - 49 = 104$, so their average is 52 and the largest is thus $52 + \frac{22}{2} = 63$. **Answer: 63**

7. Using guess and check, we find that John is 10 and his father is 30. **Answer: 10**

8. The kinetic is multiplied by the square of the velocity, or $2^2 = 4$. **Answer: 4**

9. Each place value has 5 different choices (1, 3, 5, 7, or 9) so the answer is $5 \times 5 \times 5 \times 5 = 625$. **Answer: 625**

10. If the operation is addition, there are 3 ways: $1 + 3$, $2 + 4$, or $3 + 1$.
    If the operation is subtraction, there are 5 ways: $5 - 1$, $6 - 2$, $7 - 3$, $8 - 4$, or $9 - 5$.
    If the operation is multiplication, there are 3 ways: 1×4, 2×2, 4×1
    If the operation is division, there are 2 ways: $4 \div 1$ or $8 \div 2$.
    In total, there are 13 possible ways to achieve a result of 4. There are a total of $9 \times 4 \times 9 = 324$ ways to press the buttons, so the answer is $\frac{13}{324}$. **Answer: $\frac{13}{324}$**

mathleague.org

Elementary School Sprint Test 11124

Problems 1-30

Name: _____

School: _____

Grade: _____

Correct: _____

Incorrect: _____

SCORE (4 x Correct - 1 x Incorrect) = _____

Scorer's initials: _____   Scorer's initials: _____

DO NOT BEGIN UNTIL YOU ARE INSTRUCTED TO DO SO

This round of the competition consists of 30 problems. You will have 40 minutes to complete the problems. You are <u>NOT</u> allowed to use calculators, slide rules, books, or any other aids during this round. If you are wearing a calculator wrist watch, please put it on the end of the table now. Calculations may be done on scratch paper. Record only the letter of the answer in the blanks in the right-hand column of the competition booklet. If you complete the problems before time is called, use the remaining time to check your answers.

<u>Scoring</u>: Four points will be awarded for each correct answer. One point will be deducted for each incorrect answer. No deduction is taken for skipped problems.

1. Evaluate $\sqrt{32 \times 48 + 64}$.
   A) 32   B) 40   C) 48   D) 56   E) Other

1. _____

2. How many three-digit positive integers are divisible by 6?
   A) 100   B) 120   C) 150   D) 900   E) Other

2. _____

3. What is the sum of the digits of 111111^2?
   A) 16   B) 25   C) 36   D) 39   E) Other

3. _____

4. How many digits are needed to number a 352-page book if the pages are numbered consecutively starting at 1?
   A) 948   B) 1023   C) 1026   D) 2046   E) Other

4. _____

5. What is $\frac{27 \times 27 \times 27}{3 \times 3 \times 3 \times 3}$?
   A) 27   B) 81   C) 121   D) 243   E) Other

5. _____

6. Evaluate $56 \times 1324 - 34 \times 1324$.
   A) 26480   B) 27148   C) 29362   D) 38410   E) Other

6. _____

7. The Grizzlies won 12 of their first 36 basketball games. They won the rest of their games and finished with twice as many wins as losses. How many total games did the Grizzlies compete in?
   A) 36   B) 72   C) 108   D) 144   E) Other

7. _____

8. Find $\frac{369 \times 369 \times 369}{123 \times 123 \times 3}$.
   A) 27   B) 1107   C) 3321   D) 9963   E) Other

8. _____

9. What is the greatest common divisor of the numbers 246 and 30?
   A) 2   B) 3   C) 6   D) 12   E) Other

9. _____

10. What is the median of the set $\{8, 6, 5, 3, 1\}$?
    A) 1   B) 4.6   C) 5   D) 9   E) Other

10. _____

11. Sandy's father is 34 years older than her. How old will she be when her father is twice as old as her?
    A) 9   B) 17   C) 23   D) 31   E) Other

11. _____

Elementary School Sprint Test - 11124 © 2011 mathleague.org

12. There are 300 marbles in a bowl and $\frac{1}{5}$ of them are red. 80 blue marbles are removed from the bowl. What fraction of the remaining marbles is red?
A) $\frac{1}{10}$ B) $\frac{3}{11}$ C) $\frac{4}{13}$ D) $\frac{1}{5}$ E) Other

12. _____

13. A weighted coin lands on heads $\frac{3}{5}$ of the time. What is the probability that if the coin is flipped twice, it will show heads twice?
A) $\frac{3}{5}$ B) $\frac{4}{25}$ C) $\frac{9}{25}$ D) $\frac{4}{5}$ E) Other

13. _____

14. What is the difference between the sum of the first 2011 even positive integers and the sum of the first 2011 odd positive integers?
A) 0   B) 2010!   C) 2011!   D) 2011   E) Other

14. _____

15. Two consecutive positive integers are both primes. What is the sum of their squares?
A) 4   B) 9   C) 11   D) 13   E) Other

15. _____

16. How many positive integers are divisors of the number 80?
A) 10   B) 12   C) 15   D) 18   E) Other

16. _____

17. How may zeroes does the number 41! end in?
A) 7   B) 8   C) 9   D) 10   E) Other

17. _____

18. What is the least common multiple of the numbers 8, 12, 15, and 21?
A) 240   B) 560   C) 700   D) 840   E) Other

18. _____

19. What is the product of the integers from 0 through 2011, inclusive?
A) 2011   B) 4022   C) 2010!   D) 2011!   E) Other

19. _____

20. What is the average of all 4-digit positive integers?
A) 5000   B) 5490   C) 5499.5   D) 5500   E) Other

20. _____

21. A circle has area 49π. What is the length of its circumference?
A) 7   B) 14   C) 7π D) 14π E) Other

21. _____

22. The lengths of the sides of a triangle are 8, 15, and 17. What is the area of the triangle?
A) 60   B) 120   C) 136   D) 255   E) Other

22. _____

23. The circumference and the area of a circle are numerically equal. What is the radius of the circle?

    A) 2   B) 3   C) 4   D) 5   E) Other

23. _____

24. What is the measure in degrees of the smaller angle between the hour hand and the minute hand of an analog clock at 11 : 40?

    A) 95   B) 100   C) 105   D) 110   E) Other

24. _____

25. At Fred's Fish Emporium, it costs $2.40 for a green fish, $4.50 for a red fish, and $5.65 for a yellow fish. What is the cost of 3 red fish, 1 green fish, and 2 yellow fish?

    A) $18.40   B) $24.15   C) $27.20   D) $29.70   E) Other

25. _____

26. What is the measure in degrees of each interior angle of a regular hexagon?

    A) 60   B) 90   C) 108   D) 135   E) Other

26. _____

27. 18 hens can lay 36 eggs in 4 days. How many eggs can 5 hens lay in 18 days?

    A) 18   B) 25   C) 27   D) 36   E) Other

27. _____

28. Three numbers are in the ratio $3 : 10 : 17$, and their sum is 153. What is the value of the second-largest number?

    A) 51   B) 57   C) 63   D) 81   E) Other

28. _____

29. The probability that it will be sunny on Sunday is $\frac{7}{10}$. The probability that Benny will play basketball on Sunday is $\frac{5}{9}$. If these two probabilities are independent, what is the probability that it is not sunny but Benny does play basketball?

    A) $\frac{1}{6}$ B) $\frac{2}{7}$ C) $\frac{1}{4}$ D) $\frac{1}{3}$ E) Other

29. _____

30. Andy runs at a pace of 8 minutes per mile and walks at a pace of 18 minutes per mile. He goes six miles, running for 20 minutes and then walking the rest of the way. For how many minutes does he walk?

    A) 18   B) 21   C) 28   D) 63   E) Other

30. _____

Elementary School Target Test 11124

Name: _____

Grade: _____

Team (School): _____

SCORE: # 1 _____

SCORE: # 2 _____

Scorer's initials _____   Scorer's initials _____

DO NOT BEGIN UNTIL YOU ARE INSTRUCTED TO DO SO

This round of the competition consists of eight problems. They will be presented to you in pairs. Work on one pair of the problems will be completed and answers will be collected before the next pair will be distributed. The time limit for each set of the two problems is six minutes. The first pair of problems is on the other side of this sheet. When instructed to begin, pick up your pencil and begin working. Record your final answer in the designated space on the problem sheet. All answers must be complete, legible, and simplified to lowest terms. This round allows the use of calculators, and calculations may also be done on scratch paper, but no other aids are allowed. If you complete the problems before time is called, use the time remaining to check your answers.

<u>Scoring</u>: Ten points will be awarded for each correct answer. No deduction is taken for incorrect answers or skipped problems.

1. If 1 sandwich and 1 hot dog cost a total of $6.50, how many dollars will 4 sandwiches and 4 hot dogs cost in total?

1. _____

2. How many positive odd integers have three digits?

2. _____

Name: _____

Grade: _____

Team (School): _____

SCORE: # 3 _____

SCORE: # 4 _____

Scorer's initials _____   Scorer's initials _____

DO NOT BEGIN UNTIL YOU ARE INSTRUCTED TO DO SO

The second pair of problems is on the other side of this sheet. When instructed to begin, pick up your pencil and begin working. Record your final answer in the designated space on the problem sheet. All answers must be complete, legible, and simplified to lowest terms. This round allows the use of calculators, and calculations may also be done on scratch paper, but no other aids are allowed. If you complete the problems before time is called, use the time remaining to check your answers.

Scoring: Ten points will be awarded for each correct answer. No deduction is taken for incorrect answers or skipped problems.

3. A regular six-sided die is rolled. What is the probability of rolling a prime number? Express your answer as a common fraction.

3. _____

4. The ratio of the radii of two circles is $\frac{3}{5}$. What is the ratio of their areas? Express your answer as a common fraction.

4. _____

Elementary School Target Test - 11124 © 2011 mathleague.org

Elementary School Target Test 11124

Name: _____

Grade: _____

Team (School): _____

SCORE: # 5 _____

SCORE: # 6 _____

Scorer's initials _____   Scorer's initials _____

DO NOT BEGIN UNTIL YOU ARE INSTRUCTED TO DO SO

The third pair of problems is on the other side of this sheet. When instructed to begin, pick up your pencil and begin working. Record your final answer in the designated space on the problem sheet. All answers must be complete, legible, and simplified to lowest terms. This round allows the use of calculators, and calculations may also be done on scratch paper, but no other aids are allowed. If you complete the problems before time is called, use the time remaining to check your answers.

Scoring: Ten points will be awarded for each correct answer. No deduction is taken for incorrect answers or skipped problems.

5. Evaluate the square root of the cube root of 729.

5. _____

6. A rectangle has a width of 3 and a diagonal length of 12. What is its area? Express your answer as a decimal to the nearest tenth.

6. _____

Elementary School Target Test 11124

Name: _____

Grade: _____

Team (School): _____

SCORE: # 7 _____

SCORE: # 8 _____

Scorer's initials _____   Scorer's initials _____

DO NOT BEGIN UNTIL YOU ARE INSTRUCTED TO DO SO

The fourth pair of problems is on the other side of this sheet. When instructed to begin, pick up your pencil and begin working. Record your final answer in the designated space on the problem sheet. All answers must be complete, legible, and simplified to lowest terms. This round allows the use of calculators, and calculations may also be done on scratch paper, but no other aids are allowed. If you complete the problems before time is called, use the time remaining to check your answers.

Scoring: Ten points will be awarded for each correct answer. No deduction is taken for incorrect answers or skipped problems.

7. What is the largest perfect square that is a divisor of 1372?

7. _____

8. In how many ways can 48 indistinguishable marbles be placed in a rectangular formation with no more than 20 marbles and no less than 4 marbles in a row?

8. _____

Elementary School Target Test - 11124 © 2011 mathleague.org

Elementary School Team Test 11124

Problems 1-10

Team Name: _____

School: _____

Team Members: (Captain) _____

_____

_____

_____

SCORE: _____

Scorer's Initials: _____   Scorer's Initials: _____

DO NOT BEGIN UNTIL YOU ARE INSTRUCTED TO DO SO

This round of the competition consists of 10 problems, which the team has 20 minutes to complete. Team members may work together in any way to solve the problems. Team members may talk during this section of the competition. This round allows the use of calculators, and calculations may also be done on scratch paper, but no other aids are allowed. All answers must be complete, legible, and simplified to lowest terms. The team captain must record answers on her/his own problem sheet. If the team completes the problems before time is called, use the remaining time to check your answers. Scoring: Ten points will be awarded for each correct answer. No deduction is taken for incorrect answers or skipped problems.

1. What is the sum of the first five positive integers?

        1. _____

2. Evaluate the arithmetic mean of 24 and 38.

        2. _____

3. How many hours are in 32400 seconds?

        3. _____

4. The area of a square is 256 square units. What is its perimeter in units?

        4. _____

5. Penny buys apples for a dime a dozen and sells them for one cent each. How many apples must she buy and sell to make a profit of $3?

        5. _____

6. Find $\frac{1}{2} + \frac{1}{4} + \frac{1}{8}$. Express your answer as a decimal.

        6. _____

7. Two numbers, a and b, are solutions to the equation $x^2 - 7x + 6 = 0$. Evaluate $a^2 + b^2$.

        7. _____

8. What is the tens digit of 7^{2011}?

        8. _____

9. A square has side length 4. A circle is drawn that touches all four sides of the square exactly once. What is the area of the circle? Express your answer in terms of π.

        9. _____

10. A triangle has side lengths 8, 10, and x. If x is an integer, what is the difference between the largest and smallest possible values for x?

        10. _____

Sprint

1. B
2. C
3. C
4. A
5. D
6. E
7. B
8. B
9. C
10. C
11. E
12. B
13. C
14. D
15. D
16. A
17. C
18. D
19. E
20. C
21. D
22. A
23. A
24. D
25. C
26. E
27. E
28. A
29. A
30. D

Target

1. 26
2. 450
3. $\frac{1}{2}$
4. $\frac{9}{25}$
5. 3
6. 34.9
7. 196
8. 5

Team

1. 15
2. 31
3. 9
4. 64
5. 1800
6. 0.875
7. 37
8. 4
9. 4π
10. 14

Sprint Round

1. Note that $32 = 40 - 8$ and $48 = 40 + 8$. Thus, $32 \times 48 = (40 - 8)(40 + 8) = 40^2 - 64$, so $\sqrt{32 \times 48 + 64} = 40$. **Answer: 40 (B)**

2. Every sixth integer is divisible by 6. There are $9 \times 10 \times 10 = 900$ three-digit positive integers, so $\frac{900}{6} = 150$ of them are divisible by 6. **Answer: 150 (C)**

3. $111111^2 = 12345654321$, so the sum of the digits is 36. **Answer: 36 (C)**

4. It takes 9 digits to number the 1-digit page numbers. It takes $2(90) = 180$ digits to number the 2-digit page numbers. It takes $3(253) = 759$ digits to number the 3-digit page numbers. Thus, it takes a total of 948 digits to number the book. **Answer: 948 (A)**

5. Note that $27 = 3 \times 3 \times 3$, so $\frac{27 \times 27 \times 27}{3 \times 3 \times 3 \times 3} = \frac{27 \times 27}{3} = 27 \times 9 = 243$. **Answer: 243 (D)**

6. $56 \times 1324 - 34 \times 1324 = 22 \times 1324 = 29128$. **Answer: 29128 (E)**

7. The Grizzlies lost a total of $36 - 12 = 24$ games, so they won $24 \times 2 = 48$ games. Hence, they must have played $24 + 48 = 72$ total games. **Answer: 72 (B)**

8. $\frac{369 \times 369 \times 369}{123 \times 123 \times 3} = 3 \times 3 \times 123 = 1107$. **Answer: 1107 (B)**

9. $246 = 2 \times 3 \times 41$ and $30 = 2 \times 3 \times 5$, so their greatest common divisor is $2 \times 3 = 6$. **Answer: 6 (C)**

10. The median is the middle number, or 5. **Answer: 5 (C)**

11. If Sandy's father is twice as old as Sandy, then he must be 34 years older than her. Thus, Sandy is 34 years old. **Answer: 34 (E)**

12. To start, there are $\frac{300}{5} = 60$ red marbles. There are 220 total marbles once the blue marbles are removed, so the answer is $\frac{60}{220} = \frac{3}{11}$. **Answer: $\frac{3}{11}$ (B)**

13. The probability that the coin will show heads twice is $\frac{3}{5} \times \frac{3}{5} = \frac{9}{25}$. **Answer: $\frac{9}{25}$ (C)**

14. Each even integer is 1 greater than its corresponding odd integer. Thus, the answer is $2011 \times 1 = 2011$. **Answer: 2011 (D)**

15. The only consecutive positive integers that are primes are 2 and 3. The sum of their squares is $2^2 + 3^2 = 13$. **Answer: 13 (D)**

16. $80 = 2^4 \times 5$, so 80 has $(4 + 1)(1 + 1) = 10$ divisors. **Answer: 10 (A)**

17. Each factor of 5 contributes exactly one trailing zero. There are $8 + 1 = 9$ factors of 5. **Answer: 9 (C)**

18. $8 = 2^3$, $12 = 2^2 \times 3$, $15 = 3 \times 5$, and $21 = 3 \times 7$. Thus, the least common multiple is $2^3 \times 3 \times 5 \times 7 = 840$. **Answer: 840 (D)**

19. The product includes a zero, so the total product equals 0. **Answer: 0 (E)**

20. The average of all 4-digit positive integers is the average of the first and last 4-digit positive integer. This is $\frac{1000 + 9999}{2} = 5499.5$. **Answer: 5499.5 (C)**

21. If the area is 49π, then the radius is $\sqrt{49} = 7$. Thus, the length of the circumference is $2(7)\pi = 14\pi$. **Answer: 14π (D)**

22. $8^2 + 15^2 = 17^2$, so by the Pythagorean Theorem, the triangle is a right triangle. Thus, the area is $\frac{8 \times 15}{2} = 60$. **Answer: 60 (A)**

23. We must have $\pi r^2 = 2\pi r$, or $r = 2$. **Answer: 2 (A)**

24. The minute hand is $\frac{8}{12} \times 360 = 240$ degrees past vertical. The hour hand is $330 + \frac{8}{12} \times 30 = 350$ degrees past vertical. Thus, the angle formed is $350 - 240 = 110$ degrees. **Answer: 110 (D)**

25. The answer is $3(4.50) + 2.40 + 2(5.65) = 27.20$. **Answer: \$27.20 (C)**

26. The measure of an exterior angle is $\frac{360}{6} = 60$ degrees, so the interior angle measures $180 - 60 = 120$ degrees. **Answer: 120 (E)**

27. If 18 hens can lay 36 eggs in 4 days, then 1 hen can lay 1 egg in 2 days. Thus, 5 hens lay 5 eggs in 2 days, and 5 hens lay 45 eggs in 18 days. **Answer: 45 (E)**

28. Since the numbers are in an arithmetic sequence, the second-largest number is the average of the numbers, or $\frac{153}{3} = 51$. **Answer: 51 (A)**

29. The probability is $\frac{3}{10} \times \frac{5}{9} = \frac{1}{6}$. **Answer: $\frac{1}{6}$ (A)**

30. Andy runs for $\frac{20}{8} = \frac{5}{2}$ miles, so he still has to travel $\frac{7}{2}$ miles by walking. This takes him $18 \times \frac{7}{2} = 63$ minutes. **Answer: 63 (D)**

Target Round

1. The cost is 4 times as much, or $6.5 \times 4 = 26$.
Answer: $26

2. Exactly half of the three digit positive integers are odd. The answer is $\frac{900}{2} = 450$. **Answer: 450**

3. The possible outcomes are 1, 2, 3, 4, 5, and 6. The prime outcomes are 2, 3, and 5. Thus, the desired probability is $\frac{3}{6} = \frac{1}{2}$. **Answer: $\frac{1}{2}$**

4. The ratio of their areas is the square of the ratio of the radii. This is $\left(\frac{3}{5}\right)^2 = \frac{9}{25}$. **Answer: $\frac{9}{25}$**

5. Because $9^3 = 729$, the cube root of 729 is 9. Because $3^2 = 9$, the square root of 9 is 3. **Answer: 3**

6. By the Pythagorean Theorem, the length is $\sqrt{12^2 - 3^2} = 3\sqrt{15}$. Thus, the area is $3 \times 3\sqrt{15} \approx 34.9$. **Answer: 34.9**

7. $1372 = 2^2 \times 7^3$, so its largest perfect square divisor is $2^2 \times 7^2 = 196$. **Answer: 196**

8. This is the number of factors of 48 between 4 and 20, inclusive. $48 = 2^4 \times 3$, so it has 10 positive factors. We exclude 1, 2, 3, 24, and 48 for being too large or too small. Thus, there are $10 - 5 = 5$ ways to arrange the marbles. **Answer: 5**

Team Round

1. $1 + 2 + 3 + 4 + 5 = 15$. **Answer: 15**

2. The mean is $\frac{24+38}{2} = 31$. **Answer: 31**

3. There are $60 \times 60 = 3600$ seconds in one hour, so there are $\frac{32400}{3600} = 9$ hours in 32400 seconds. **Answer: 9**

4. The side length of the square is $\sqrt{256} = 16$ units, so the perimeter is $4 \times 16 = 64$ units. **Answer: 64**

5. For each dozen apples she buys and sells, Penny earns $12 - 10 = 2$ cents. She needs to make this profit 150 times over, so she must sell $150 \times 12 = 1800$ apples. **Answer: 1800**

6. $\frac{1}{2} + \frac{1}{4} + \frac{1}{8} = \frac{7}{8}$, or 0.875. **Answer: 0.875**

7. By Vieta's Formulas, $a + b = 7$ and $ab = 6$. But $a^2 + b^2 = (a + b)^2 - 2ab = 7^2 - 12 = 37$. **Answer: 37**

8. Note that $7^1 = 7$, $7^2 = 49$, $7^3 = 343$, and $7^4 = 2401$. Thus, the tens digit cycles modulo 4, and the tens digit of 7^{2011} is that of 7^3. The answer is 4. **Answer: 4**

9. The diameter of the circle is the side length of the square, so the radius of the circle is 2. Thus, the area of the circle is $2^2 \times \pi = 4\pi$. **Answer: 4π**

10. By the Triangle Inequality, the largest possible value for x is 17 and the smallest possible value for x is 3. The difference is $17 - 3 = 14$. **Answer: 14**